TEACHING THE BASICS OF THEORY OF MIND

by the same author

Teaching Theory of Mind
A Curriculum for Children with High
Functioning Autism, Asperger's Syndrome,
and Related Social Challenges
Kirstina Ordetx
Foreword by Susan J. Moreno
ISBN 978 1 84905 897 1

TEACHING THE BASICS OF THEORY OF MIND

A Complete Curriculum with Supporting Materials for Children with Autism Spectrum Disorder and Related Social Difficulties Aged Approximately 5 to 9 Years

KIRSTINA ORDETX

Jessica Kingsley Publishers
London and Philadelphia

First published in 2015
This edition published in 2018
by Jessica Kingsley Publishers
73 Collier Street
London N1 9BE, UK
and
400 Market Street, Suite 400
Philadelphia, PA 19106, USA

www.jkp.com

Library of Congress Cataloging in Publication Data
A CIP catalog record for this book is available from the Library of Congress

British Library Cataloguing in Publication Data
A CIP catalogue record for this book is available from the British Library

ISBN 978 1 78775 036 4
eISBN 978 0 85700 952 4

Printed and bound in the United States

CONTENTS

PREFACE

After years of providing social skills training to children who have difficulty grasping the most primal social concepts, I realized that it was one thing to teach them what to say and do in certain situations, but it was entirely another thing to help them to truly understand "why." The conception of theory of mind (ToM) and the writings of Simon Baron-Cohen and colleagues have intrigued me for years. Once I had immersed myself into this theory, it became more apparent to me that, as practitioners, many of us in the field of autism treatment have been implementing skill training while missing the core elements. In my own practice, I have been addressing a diverse range of perceptual development skills, focusing on joint ToM training. I have found the use of cognitive behavior therapy (CBT) as a primary approach to instruction to have a profound impact on many of my pediatric and adult clients who have been identified with challenges in social learning and relatedness.

After writing *Teaching Theory of Mind: A Curriculum for Children with High Functioning Autism, Asperger's Syndrome, and Related Social Challenges* (Ordetx 2012), I began to develop more activities for use with a younger population of children who were affected by symptoms related to autism, hyperactivity, sensory dysfunction, and language processing problems. This manual highlights the earliest stages of social development and the foundation that is critical to later social and communication functioning.

This manual may be used as a prerequisite to the *Teaching Theory of Mind: A Curriculum for Children with High Functioning Autism, Asperger's Syndrome, and Related Social Challenges* (Ordetx 2012) manual, as the activities are designed to target a much younger audience with the goal to build a foundation of skills that have been associated with ToM. The curriculum targets children aged 5–9 in the hope that the skill-deficit gap does not widen with age. More recent studies are emphasizing the obvious impairments of early skills such as imitation, joint attention, pretend play, language, self-regulation, and metacognition in children who have social-communication delays. The importance of teaching these skills must not be understated, but rather underscored both within the clinic and the child's natural routine. We cannot wait to address these delays until they fully emerge in the elementary or middle school years. These are the basics…the fundamental building blocks of a child's social cognition, and, in some cases, the catalyst to independence in adulthood. I have found these activities to be very useful with a younger population in my own practice and hope that it will support enhanced social development for many others, enlightening their future relationships, self-confidence, and perception of their social world.

I wish you the best of luck in your future endeavors for our children.

Kirstina Ordetx Ed.D.

INTRODUCTION

This manual provides a 12-week curriculum designed to incorporate a multi-sensory approach to developing the critical, basic aspects of ToM. It has been created as a mate to *Teaching Theory of Mind: A Curriculum for Children with High Functioning Autism, Asperger's Syndrome, and Related Social Challenges* (Ordetx 2012), which was written to provide a curriculum for children and adolescents, aged 7–16. The layout of both manuals is consistent to allow for the instructor to gain a sense of routine in curriculum provision across both programs. The approach incorporates the same principles of CBT to establish a framework for successful skill acquisition. The trainer's role is both a teacher and facilitator to enhance the student's awareness of self-motivation in social situations. It is intended for use in a small group setting with children aged 5–9 who have been diagnosed with autism spectrum disorder and related social difficulties or attention/sensory-based conditions. Although I recognize that there are several quality social skills training programs available (and many of them are listed at the end of this manual), I have stumbled across a roadblock with some of my clients who are not ready for more advanced, sophisticated ToM concepts and language. By providing them with a very simple and clear presentation of the basic concepts in the first activity manual, I have been able to successfully prepare them for these other resources, character stories, and supplemental ToM training materials.

This manual has been prepared to address very early concepts that may lead to enhanced social development. The curriculum may be taught by a variety of professionals, including teachers, speech/language pathologists, psychologists, behavior therapists, and guidance counselors. Professionals who intend to teach this curriculum should gain a solid understanding of the development of ToM and each participant's diagnoses and comorbid symptoms when applicable. There is a wealth of resources that will reinforce and extend the teachings of this curriculum. Therefore, readers are encouraged to seek references from the list provided at the end of the manual to supplement the curriculum and provide additional research and information related to early social development and topics of related interest.

The curriculum is the primary focus of interest in this manual. Each section in this manual will highlight 1 of the 12 sessions in this training series and has been organized to provide the following information:

- target skill

- instructional relevance

- materials list

- activities

- cognitive behavioral concentration

- caregiver letters.

All Appendix pages and card sets mentioned in materials lists and marked ✓ can be photocopied or downloaded to print from https://library.jkp.com/redeem using the code FUOHEZE.

TARGET POPULATION

The curriculum has been designed to enhance the development of ToM and subsequently enhance social understanding in children who demonstrate challenges with prerequisite skills that lead to successful social relationships and situations. The literature suggests ToM training to be beneficial for children who have been diagnosed with the following:

- autism spectrum disorder (ASD)

- Asperger's syndrome (AS)

- high-functioning autism (HFA)

- pervasive developmental disorder—not otherwise specified (PDD-NOS)

- non-verbal learning disorder (NVLD)

- attention deficit disorder (ADD)

- attention deficit hyperactivity disorder (ADHD)

- receptive-expressive language disorder (RELD)

- social anxiety

- sensory integration dysfunction (SID).

In this manual, ASD, AS, HFA, and PDD will all be referred to as autism spectrum conditions. All other listed conditions will be referred to as attention/sensory-based conditions. This is for the purpose of simplicity and is not suggestive of diagnostic labeling.

ROLE OF EARLY DEVELOPMENT IN SOCIAL EFFICACY

The window of development from infancy through year four provides a child with significant advances in psychological understanding. Within the first year of life, a child's appreciation of self and others is cultivated with every act of shared attention. The infant learns quickly to read a partner's facial expressions to seek clues that will help him to respond in familiar and unfamiliar situations. These exchanges occur spontaneously and build through observational learning. They happen multiple times per day and are dynamically diverse across settings, partners, and conditions. They are the strong roots of the ever-expanding social tree. From this foundation, the child begins to define himself by his likes, dislikes, and abilities. He shares an understanding of the world with others. He becomes a more competent social partner through emerging self-understanding and self-confidence.

Conversations are nurtured and set the stage for pre-literacy skills, language, and cognitive development. The child becomes more mindful of his social surroundings and demonstrates an increased ability to manage his impulses, emotions, and desires. He develops a propensity for both cooperation and conflict resolution. Through this span of early, typical development, the child's awareness of the hidden psychological states or mental states of others is enriched. Research continues to support the evidence of early red flags in development and encourages focused instruction to target gaps in early social development. It is my hope that a focus on this type of early intervention might have an influence on the child's social responsiveness, competence, and ability to develop relationships across the lifespan.

IMITATION

Imitation skills emerge early in a typical child's development and serve the functions of learning and socialization. Reciprocal imitation provides a framework for early peer interactions and allows for young children to exchange non-verbal communication during play (Ingersoll 2008). Social imitation is one of the hallmark deficits of autism and is likely somewhat responsible for the lack of development of social-communication skills, including receptive language and joint attention. Imitation continues to have a profound effect on the development of social communication and relationships throughout a child's life. The direct impact of imitation on language development and ToM is evident. Through these powerful exchanges, an infant is able to coordinate eye contact and vocalizations, while responding to and often imitating changes in the adult partner's facial expressions. As the infant connects with various partners, he recognizes critical affective cues and begins to regulate his own behavior to please or alter his partner's emotional response. It is here, in these early stages of social development where autism may become evident, as the child does not exhibit an ability to synchronize with a partner. According to Gopnik and Meltzoff (1994), imitation also allows for acquisition of a "like me" state, which activates the infant's awareness of self and others.

Exciting research on the role that imitation may play as a predictor of ToM is currently in progress. The ability to imitate or "mirror" another person's actions is thought to be driven by mirror neurons in the brain. Mirror neurons fire and allow for imitation to occur, leading to the acquisition of new skills and a foundation for detecting, predicting, and understanding the intentions of others. Studies comparing children with HFA and typically developing children indicate lower activity in the mirror neurons of autism (Iacoboni *et al.* 1999). Mirroring may be at the core of social cognition, allowing the brain to acquire and process information that leads to understanding other people's actions, intentions, and goals (Marsh and Hamilton 2011). When the mirror neurons fail to create this experience for the infant, later social challenges may follow, as suggested in Ramachandran and Oberman's "Broken Mirror Theory" (2006). This theory outlines the parallels between the social deficits in autism and the role of mirror neurons. Iacoboni *et al.* (1999) further advise that imitation is vital in the development of conventional social cognition and makes it possible for the child to foster empathy. Other studies are also shedding light on the significance of imitation in autism (Lord 1995; Stone and Yoder 2001). Rogers *et al.* (2003) demonstrated a significant correlation between social reciprocity and early imitation performance in follow-up studies.

Imitation lays a framework for the young child to understand intentionality—that another person's actions are goal-directed. This is recognized early in development when the child observes and uses proto-declarative pointing. In addition, imitation allows for the reading of non-verbal communication, gestures, social referencing, and co-regulation. Co-regulation provides a natural ability to anticipate and respond to a partner, which allows the child to respond appropriately to turns in reciprocal actions and vocalizations. Initially, the child observes and imitates novel actions. Following this skill development is the child's ability to exhibit delayed imitation and recall earlier observations. These critical elements of early development occur from 12 weeks to nine months of age and generate an expansive repertoire of learned actions (Neilsen and Dissanayake 2004). These skills have been long recognized as devoid or significantly impaired in the early development of many children who have been diagnosed with autism spectrum or sensory/attention-based conditions. This impairment in imitation early in infancy and toddlerhood may be a useful predictor of later privation of ToM (Goldman 2006).

Imitation stands out as a source from which more sophisticated social development and competency emerges in early childhood. Few would argue that it is fundamental to human development, social learning, and the recognition of culture in society. It is during these experiences with imitation in early childhood that the child recognizes that he is like another person. As imitation progresses, the child also learns that he is different from another person. Studies indicate that this "like me/ not like me" recognition may not occur in the brain when autism is present (Lombardo *et al.* 2010). Although further research is needed to confirm the role of mirror neurons, imitation, and the function of neural responses in children who have autism, the available information provides insight into early impairments that may be critical in the development of later social competence. It would seem necessary for practitioners to place an emphasis on the early teachings of imitation skills to children with autism in an effort to lay the foundation for future social cognition and relationship development. Successful dyadic interactions lead to triadic interactions, or what is referred to as "joint attention."

JOINT ATTENTION

Joint attention encompasses the ability to follow the direction of a partner's eye gaze and to coordinate a back and forth reciprocation of attention to an object or event of interest. Consider how an infant integrates his attention during a simple game of "peek-a-boo." He recognizes the social bid from a parent and then, in turn, matches this bid with his own purposeful behaviors, which might include a smile, a giggle, and his own eye gaze. He will then engage in further skills, such as timing, sustained attention, and recognition of facial expressions. These abilities all develop within the first year of a child's typical development and are driven by the natural reinforcement of intrinsic and social pleasure.

Langdell's (1978) studies suggest that recognition of faces plays a crucial role in the development of social communication. Children who lack ToM development are likely deficient in the area of social cognition and particularly in joint attention. Videotapes from first birthday parties of typical children and those who were later diagnosed with autism shed some interesting insight into this critical area of social development. The lack of attention to the faces of others was evident in the videos and may have actually been a predictor of later diagnoses in some of the children (Osterling and Dawson 1994). Due to a thwart in the early development of recognition of the face, later joint attention tasks may subsequently be hindered. Children with autism will likely demonstrate delays in their ability to shift gaze to regulate turn taking in social situations such as beginning conversations and in popular, reciprocal games that are typical of early child development (i.e. "peek-a-boo").

Joint attention consists of the child's demonstration of the ability to both initiate and respond to joint attention. The child will use eye contact or gestures (such as pointing) to bring the partner's attention to herself, another person, or an object of interest. Even before a child can say the word "airplane," she will call a partner's attention to it by pointing and looking at it. As a result, the partner looks at the airplane, shares a facial expression, and comments, "Yes, I see the airplane, too!" The child may attempt to say "airplane," to which the partner will exhibit delight and the child's behavior is reinforced. In this brief example, the young child receives both social pleasure and learns language. It is this ability to initiate joint attention that is considered one of the hallmark deficits of social development for children with autism. To describe the ability to respond to joint attention, we could simply reverse this same scenario. Rather, it would begin with the partner calling attention to the airplane via eye gaze or a gesture. The child's ability to follow these cues is an example of responding to joint attention (Mundy and Newell 2007). Later, the child will develop an ability to shift his gaze across several partners and call attention to self or an object within a group. This skill becomes more complex over time and involves the child's careful monitoring of the non-verbal behaviors of others. It will continue to serve as a foundation for learning communication, play development, and eventually lead to conversations about a topic. For the young child, joint attention becomes a pivotal skill in the development of social language.

LANGUAGE

The joint attention of two people makes pretend play and precipitous language acquisition possible (Frith and Frith 2003). The development of language, imitation, and observed learning seem to go hand-in-hand. The child's ability to absorb actions, emotions, and words and re-coordinate them to produce their own is referred to as "simulation" (Press, Richardson, and Bird 2010). The introduction of triadic joint attention is another catalyst for the growth of the infant's vocabulary. In triadic joint attention, the child directs his gaze toward an object and then to a partner. When an infant shares this type of attention with an adult, this serves as an invitation for the adult to label the object that the child has identified with his eyes. Children acknowledge this reinforcement and continue to initiate adults with their gaze direction. Adults respond with consistent labels and the child builds an ever-growing repertoire of vocabulary. If imitation and joint attention contribute to the development of language, then the phenomenon of a "language explosion" when the child enters a social environment, like daycare or preschool, would be easily explained. The steady exposure to multiple communicative partners, consistent observation, and imitation of others' social behavior would account for an acceleration in all aspects of typical language development.

Experience with the autism spectrum highlights a pervasive difference in the use of pointing, joint attention, and early vocalizations in comparison with the typical ages and stages of development (Charman *et al.* 2000). Pointing is in itself an impressive and critical indicator of early language. Used in two primary ways, pointing may be proto-imperative (the index finger is extended in order to make a request) or proto-declarative (the index finger is extended in order to call a partner's attention to something). After a child successfully uses pointing and recognizes the pointing of others as a highly reinforcing means of functional and social communication, he will coordinate his point with a more sustained gaze and, eventually, a shift in attention across multiple partners and objects. The development of this set of skills seems to be an obvious pioneer into the world of reciprocal conversation. In addition, the child's sustained attention allows for important social language to be learned, including the imitation of facial expressions, linguistic structures, and empathy (Rogers *et al.* 2003).

Wulff (1985) suggests that the weak interpersonal communication skills that are characteristic in autism spectrum conditions may be a result of limited early experiences in sharing and engaging with others. Many children with a spectrum condition are able to effectively initiate communication for the purpose of satisfying their basic wants and needs. Although they successfully master the ability to make requests, other functions of communication, including commenting, question asking, and social reciprocation, may remain impaired or absent (Wetherby and Prutting 1984). The idiosyncratic style of communication in autism is evident. However, in typical development, language rapidly builds upon this social foundation and eventually leads to complex interactions that are largely non-verbal and conversational. Consider a scenario where a person walks into a room and a conversation is in progress. The person will monitor various features of the conversation, such as voice volume, posture, topic and social dominance, and will then modify his own behavior to align it with the group. This intricate process is not explicitly taught in childhood, but rather assumed from social observation, imitation, and language development and is a vital factor in determining social acceptance.

We clearly see the consequence of language development deficits surface for adolescents on the spectrum. The inability to shift and demonstrate this type of flexible thinking leaves the older child unaware of what is being fully communicated around him both verbally and non-verbally. Subsequently, he is oblivious to his partner's intentions and a significant breakdown in social comprehension will occur. Although not commonly recognized in the earlier years of children who are considered "high functioning," this example is commonly portrayed in a parent's reports that the adolescent has difficulty making/keeping friends, participating in conversations, is one-sided in communicating with others, or demonstrates weak comprehension of social-pragmatic language skills. By three years of age, the typically developing child is actively acquiring and using language to describe mental states, such as verbs that describe knowledge, thoughts, feelings, and desires. Failure to assimilate such language will likely prevent a child from performing well on later mental reasoning tasks. This is consistent with the early development of children who have been diagnosed with autism and may serve as an early warning sign. Comprehensive assessments of labeling may identify impairments in social language. Should the child be deficient in a repertoire of social labels and their meaning, we may surmise that social and pretend play will be compromised.

PLAY

Pretend play may provide another early indicator of ToM (Leslie 1987). The absence of imagination in play is commonly highlighted as a diagnostic feature of autism spectrum conditions. Experiential observations suggest that there is an evident lack of motivation for these children to engage in role relationships. Although we may see children observing others in play or initiating a partner, their participation is likely to wane as play becomes more abstract and complex. Professionals frequently call attention to the weakness of abstract thought processes across the spectrum. Imagination and creative thought are managed in the same part of the brain as abstract thinking. It is here that we often see the prevalent complaints of symptomology emerge in early childhood. Imagination allows for the child to think about, recreate, or experience a state of pretense. This occurs in the absence of visual representation. Imagination is consistently enhanced when the young child listens intently to fairy tales and fantasy-based stories. The important development here lies in the big picture, which is acquiring an understanding of the integration of make-believe characters, worlds, and endings, rather than simply memorizing the text. Imagining requires thinking that is counterfactual, or rather a substitution for what is real. This ability to employ the abstract in pretend play is a key element of social development (Leslie 1987). When we take into account that spectrum conditions are further characterized by a concrete, literal-thinking style, the developmental incongruence seems to be evident. Considering that the absence of pretend play is a hallmark feature of autism spectrum conditions, yet is a critical contributor to a child's social development, gaining an understanding of the evolution of imagination and play would seem essential (Wulff 1985).

Watch children engage in pretend play and you will witness anything but reality. From mud pies that taste delicious to a stick used as a magical wand, pretend play allows for the child's imagination to take flight. Although this may seem like simple child's play, theorists have credited the hierarchy of play skills as the foundation of socialization, cognition, and self-regulation (Kanter 2006). Piaget (1962) in his *Play, Dreams, and Imitation in Childhood*, expressed the critical significance of play in the development of intelligence. She further attributes pretend play to the child's ability to switch perspectives. Perspective taking develops in play when the child demonstrates the capacity to create and shift roles. Roles are assigned in pretend play as a result of the child's keen attention to her identity of herself, the status of others within the family or community, and the interaction of these multiple relationships within a social context. Pretend play is dynamic. The child reveals a natural flexibility to assign and reassign relationships according to a variety of circumstances. In pretend play scenarios, the child models emotional experiences by attributing representational characteristics to dramatic roles such as mood, voice, and posture. A pretend character may represent an actual, familiar person, a story character, or a combination of both. Pretend play is complex. The child is required to assimilate and accommodate known information while simultaneously integrating a theme that contradicts real life. This intricate stage of play development is where we observe the child's acquisition of critical life skills including planning, problem-solving, organization, storytelling, reasoning, and assessment.

Vygotsky (1967) agreed that pretend play signifies a meaningful transition from a primarily concrete to more abstract demonstration of executive functioning. Initially, the infant explores toys in a realm of functional play. These physical, sensory-based explorations of objects for their actual use are referred to as primary representations. They provide the child with a concrete understanding of object manipulation. Between 18 and 24 months of age, the child will demonstrate the ability to use an object to represent something else. For example, in the absence of a cup, the child may use a block to take a "drink." Other mental representations of pretend play may extend the theme as the child "pours" milk from another block into the "cup." To demonstrate the social congruence of pretend play, we know that a peer might extend another block and request for the child to pour him a "drink" also. By aged two and a half, imagination dominates play behavior and the child's evolving capacity for representation develops into meta-representations (Leslie 1987). Consider the integration of concepts in the basis for the following play theme:

- Categorical knowledge leads the child to choose a theme for play: birthday party.

- Object representation prompts the child to select actual and pretend objects to symbolize a cake, plates, candles, presents, and people.

- Planning and organization allow for the child to direct an appropriate sequence of actions to create a party.

- Memory is evident as the child assigns details to the party that may have personal significance (i.e. grandparents arrive, cake is yellow with flowers).

- Mental states are assigned to each character (actual or imaginary), as they reveal feelings, intentions, and desires.

Prior to the emergence of pretend play, the preschool aged child engages in egocentric thinking and play. Egocentrism is a term used to describe the young child's inability to see things from another person's point of view. People may describe children in this age group by saying, "The world revolves around her." Step inside of the child's mind and one can see that this is true from her perspective and this perspective is the only one that is taken into account. Piaget (1962) believed that egocentrism eventually comes to an end when cognitive maturity and exposure to voluminous social experiences have been encountered. It is important to draw attention to the similarity between egocentrism and the general description of the social deficits across the spectrum. The consequence here is evident in the way that egocentrism impacts the child's cognitive reasoning and social interactions. This is consistent with the diagnostic criteria for this condition and the historical concerns related to social development across the lifespan. Since ToM is heavily based on the child's ability to occupy another person's point of view, then it would seem logical to link the importance of early imitation and imaginative play to the development of ToM.

THEORY OF MIND

"Theory of Mind" (ToM) was a term introduced by Premack and Woodruff (1978) to describe ways in which we understand and interpret our social world. It is defined as "the ability to make inferences about another's representational states and to predict behavior accordingly" (Lewis and Mitchell 2014, p.2). Also referred to as "mind-reading" and "social referencing," it provides an examination of the intricate system of observing social cues, which seem so effortless in typical social development (Baron-Cohen 2001; Striano and Rochat 2000). Imagine trying to interact with someone without being able to assume their thoughts, feelings, or beliefs. ToM gives us insight to learning about others without exchanging a single word. Our ability to engage ToM is dependent on the quad-senses: seeing, hearing, thinking, and feeling.

- **Seeing** allows us to use our eyes to observe other people, their interactions with us and with others, too. It provides us with a detector of details because every movement and expression leads us to interpret something social, right down to the eyebrows. Think about a neutral facial expression, which could be interpreted as a feeling of surprise if the eyebrows are lifted or a feeling of anger if the eyebrows are narrowed. Seeing also lends to our perception of our social environment. We notice movement, comings and goings, additions and subtractions to social scenarios. Our eyes allow us to notice every small, seemingly insignificant aspect that can completely change everything. Seeing is critical to early childhood learning wherein observation of others leads to imitation and the mastery of developmental stages. Seeing is the catalyst for assessing social situations, initiating problem-solving strategies, and assuming an appropriate role within a group. Seeing leads to thinking, believing, and knowing.

- **Hearing** provides us with the ability to hear not just what is being said, but how it is being said. Our ears are keen to listen for changes in voice volume, pitch, intonation, and rhythm. When a messenger changes one simple word in a sentence, it can alter the meaning altogether. For example, asking "*You* want popcorn?" or "You want *popcorn*?" conveys two different messages. By attending to the paralinguistic cues, the listener can truly hear the message and respond appropriately.

- **Thinking** is a complex and abstract concept for children who have not developed ToM. Thinking is very different than knowing and allows for the personalization of information. What you think about something may not be the same as what someone else thinks. Thinking can be changed by our beliefs, as we attempt to make predictions based on previous experiences, literature, and facts. If we *believe* that a busy road is a place to avoid based on stories our parents have told, being witness to an accident, or rules, then we will *think* that it is dangerous. Thinking is further altered by our imagination and consideration of possibilities.

- **Feeling** is another abstract notion involving a conscious state of alertness or emotion. A person must be responsive and sensitive to these intrinsic reactions to people, places, and things. Feelings are generated from experiences and are interpreted and expressed differently across people, making them even more challenging to interpret or even recognize for individuals who lack ToM.

Researchers suggest that ToM occurs in typical development around a child's fourth year and becomes second nature by age five. This is supported by a series of clinical trials referred to as "false belief" tests (Wimmer and Perner 1983; Perner, Leekam, and Wimmer 1987; Gopnik and Astington 1988). However, studies indicate that children can recognize some of the mental states prior to age four, such as a partner's intentions, desires, some feelings, and seeing (Leslie and Frith 1988; Astington and Jenkins 1999; Wellman 1990; Baron-Cohen, Leslie, and Frith 1986). Prior to this age, children presume that others think the way that they (self) think, feel the way that they feel, and believe the same things that they believe. They assume that others have the same opinions and beliefs as their own. They view the world as it relates to the self and what is seen (Epley, Morewedge and Keysar 2004). We have previously referred to this as egocentrism. Wimmer and Perner designed a series of tests to assess these mental states of simple beliefs. The first order belief test analyzes what a person believes about what another person knows. It is highly recommended that Social Experience instructors should delve into the research and procedures for testing for false belief.

Experience and research indicates that many children who are diagnosed with a spectrum condition are unable to observe and interpret non-verbal social clues to mentally simulate what another person is thinking, feeling, or planning. Uta Frith (2012) refers to this ability to mentalize as a core obstacle in social development for children with autism and Asperger's syndrome. Consider the following example: Jacob is walking through the woods. He sees a long, curved stick and jumps back with a fearful look on his face. We know that Jacob jumped, not because he actually saw a snake, but because he believed that there might have been a snake. His belief led to his reaction. Although this notion that a person's beliefs and wants will determine his behavior seems completely predictable, the mental states of what Jacob *thinks*, *knows*, and *feels* are unobservable. To predict his actions, we must be able to put ourselves in his shoes. This also requires that we consider the clues that we are given. He is in a forest. There is a stick on the ground. It is curved. He looks scared.

Consider another example, wherein clues are critical in predicting the behavior of another person: Michael is reaching for his hat. If that is all of the information that we have been given, then we have many questions to ponder. Will he put the hat on? Will he give the hat to his brother? Will he put it in the closet? The clues of the scenario will be important. If his body is facing a mirror, we might assume that he will put the hat on. If his brother is standing near him with his arm extended, we may assume that he will hand the hat to his brother. If he is moving in the direction of the closet, we might assume that he will put the hat away. These are simple examples of how important clues become in real life, social situations and also in literature.

Every minute of a child's social day is filled with shifting. This ability to spontaneously and automatically monitor information allows for successful interactions and responses to people. We give careful spatial attention to details that are specific to a setting, person, or situation in an effort to stay in sync with our world. We look for clues that are both observable and surmised. By four months of age, a developmental phenomenon is occurring, which allows for the child to engage in facial and emotional recognition in people. Studies have suggested that an impairment in eye gaze perception is present early in autism and may contribute to later consequences in social communication (Leekam *et al.* 1997; Grice *et al.* 2005). Children who have autism spectrum conditions are often observed exhibiting gaze aversion and fleeting attention, which may further impair social advancement.

The importance of visual cognition in social development seems evident. It is one, basic skill in an impressive collection of functional and organizational skills. These skills make the child's actions goal-directed and are referred to as executive functioning skills or metacognition.

METACOGNITION

Metacognition is an awareness of one's own process of thinking. In other words, it is our ability to think about how we think. Also referred to as executive functioning, it has been cited as the most important contributor to a child's emotional and behavioral engagement in the school setting (Jahroni *et al.* 2013). In the above scenarios, we applied a process to our thinking. We supported our predictions about the behavior of Jacob and Michael, through the use of clues, reasoning, inferencing, and working memory. We might consider our own experiences in such situations and compare them to a variety of possibilities. Metacognition involves a variety of skills including planning (how will I think), monitoring (how my thinking is actually going), repairing (do I need to fix or change my plan), and evaluating (how did I do). It is clear that this intricate process requires the ability to apply flexible thinking. Flexible thinking is an executive function of the brain, which allows for the child to shift his thinking and consider various possibilities. Children who exhibit flexible thinking are also able to adapt to changes in social situations and shift when unexpected transitions occur in verbal or non-verbal exchanges. Although metacognition and executive functioning skills are often referred to in the context of academic performance, the link between them and social cognition must be acknowledged in the big picture leading to the development of ToM.

Weak metacognition skills will dually surface as problematic when the young child begins to read chapter books. As literary requirements transition from books based on pictures and facts to the more abstract development of fictional characters, children who present with limited metacognition and ToM may exhibit deterioration in reading performance. This book provides a section of activities to enhance metacognition in early reading comprehension.

Metacognition is also termed "self-regulation" or "self-regulated learning." However, we might consider several types of regulation as they relate to social development. Regulation might be related to thought, emotion, or socialization. In all three cases, the child would demonstrate regulation by appropriately controlling and adapting his responses to the stimuli of a given situation. When the child's responses are coordinated with his social partner's behaviors, a harmony exists that we might refer to as "matching."

SELF-REGULATION

Children take in an overwhelming amount of sensory stimulation every day. Sights, sounds, movement, and smells are ever-changing and often unpredictable. Typically, the child's brain will receive this information, filter it, and process it accordingly. The body will regulate and respond accordingly (Ramachandran and Oberman 2006). The role of self-regulation in pretend play was described by Ossorio (2006) as important to the child's ability to assess, evaluate, modify, and act in a way that would be considered "matching" to onlookers.

Deficits in self and social regulation are highlighted in the diagnostic criteria of autism and may be observed in children who present with attention/sensory-based conditions. The child's behavior may represent an obvious under-reaction or over-reaction to stimuli and ultimately appears disorganized. In addition, the child may be unable to re-establish a balance following a period of elevated arousal or in response to stress (Loveland 2005). This inability to find a "just right" or "matching" state may lead to odd or unexpected behaviors, increasing the child's vulnerability to social problems and peer conviction. There are several resources listed in the appendix that can offer support in the explicit instruction of self-regulation.

WHY TEACH THEORY OF MIND?

Frith (2012) suggests that the inability to "mentalize" is the core shortcoming of autism. Mentalizing refers to the ability to perceive and interpret the mental states of others including what they think, know, believe, feel, desire, and intend. Unlike concrete concepts, which are areas of strength for children with autism spectrum conditions, the interpretation of the thoughts, feelings, and ever-changing behaviors of others is a far more abstract and transient concept. For these children, the ability to read social cues does not come naturally and must be explicitly taught. It is important to teach ToM for many reasons.

The developmental issues that have been discussed in this manual pose a cause for concern related to the trajectory of social skill development and cognition in children who have autism spectrum and attention/sensory-based conditions. Research indicates a high treatment prevalence of anxiety and mood disorders in children who were diagnosed earlier with Asperger's syndrome or HFA (Kim *et al.* 2000). Real-life social experiences are complex. They require flexibility, shifting, and an intricate integration of common-sense skills. However, we find that these skills may not come naturally in development under the spectrum of autism and that the deficits found in early development may provide explanation to the bigger question of ToM.

THE FUTURE OF THEORY OF MIND RESEARCH

The positive outlook in the development of social aptitude lies in the convergence between research and intervention. Recent and future studies are focusing on the relationship between cognition and the brain in the course of development. The findings may offer insight to explain how and when autism symptoms manifest in early childhood. It would seem appropriate to approach treatment from a preventative perspective. If we assume that children with autism do not have an absence of these skill capabilities, but rather a lower response to stimuli to acquire them, then intervention would hold strong merit for the habilitation of early childhood developmental milestones, metacognition, and ToM. The consideration of the typical stages of a child's development in socialization and language becomes paramount if we are to effectively address these central impairments.

ToM is more commonly investigated in the fields of developmental psychology, cognitive neuroscience, and child development. The research remains cutting-edge and does not yet explain all of the aspects of social impairments. It is not exempt from criticism and does not mold well into a behavior analytic framework, where autism treatment is widely established. However, it is continually uncovering more information to help us to gain a more refined understanding of the fundamental challenges that children have in understanding and navigating the social world. In the meantime, we should embrace and challenge new findings while recognizing the value in our "thought science" or clinical observations that have led us to identify the key features of early social challenges. Our obligation then, is to integrate research with practice to provide effective and lasting interventions that aim to bridge the gap in the child's social development.

HOW TO HELP CHILDREN WHO ARE NOT READY FOR THIS CURRICULUM

Careful observation and assessment of prospective participants will lend to more successful groupings and subsequent learning outcomes. There will be many children who do not demonstrate readiness for this and other types of ToM curricula. One or more of the following realities may prevent them from being a candidate:

- chronological age

- developmental age

- attention

- behavior

- ability to learn in a group setting.

In many cases, the child may benefit from a more discrete form of instruction, fewer distractions, or modified curriculum.

ABOUT THE CURRICULUM

This curriculum was developed to provide a basic, primary-level series of lessons to address ToM as a whole "experience" of social development. The experience of being social is multi-faceted and ever-changing and requires the child to learn to integrate an assortment of skills, rather than apply one skill at a time. Traditionally, professionals and parents who are aware of the child's social deficits have found it challenging to establish a distinction between addressing social skills (what to do), social cognition (what to know), social awareness (when to apply it), and social understanding (why to apply it). Because there is no true "mastery" of being social, this curriculum focuses on building a social foundation, as if with building blocks. Participants will be encouraged to utilize learned skills outside of this program, which will allow their Social Experience to continue to evolve through problem-solving, self-assessment, and the use of effective repair strategies.

This 12-week curriculum offers a practical and easy-to-implement series of lessons which are designed to target the basic, core concepts of social development and are filled with simple terminology and kinesthetic learning activities. When children are carefully placed in groups, the groups themselves provide an essential element of the process. I have found that success increases with group management and attention to each, individual participant.

Groups should be made up of four to six children. Each session's content will require approximately 60 minutes to complete instruction. Sessions may be conducted in a quiet clinic setting and should be free from distractions. The instructor will only need enough space for the group to sit comfortably and to set up and view video samples. I typically offer my groups a choice to sit in chairs or on the floor. The floor seems to create a less formal setting and is more comparable to a game play scenario.

WHAT TO TEACH

The essential skills which lead to enhanced social success and ToM development are covered in this manual, including the necessary foundation skills.

THE SOCIAL EXPERIENCE: FOUNDATION SKILLS

- **Joint attention:** The child's ability to initiate, reciprocate, and maintain interactive eye gaze, gestures, and attention-gaining strategies.

- **Imitation:** The child's ability to learn and replicate the actions of others.

- **Identification:** The child's recognition of labels for emotions and ability to discriminate emotional cues across people and self.

- **Eye gaze detection:** The child's ability to follow the direction of a person's eyes to identify what the person wants or is thinking about.

- **Point of view:** The child's ability to recognize that other people may have the same or different likes and dislikes, feelings, and reactions to the same thing(s).

- **Predictions:** The child's ability to make guesses or infer by looking at pictures, text, or other clues.

- **Checking in:** The child's ability to read a partner's face frequently during social interactions and to alter behavior based on the partner's behavior.

- **Social queries:** The child's ability to ask questions for the purpose of gaining social information to learn more about a social partner.

- **Matching behavior:** The child's ability to recognize when his own behavior or another person's behavior is an appropriate match for the situation.

- **Self-assessment:** The child's ability to recognize and evaluate his own behavior to make modifications that will lead to social learning growth and success.

WHY COGNITIVE BEHAVIOR THERAPY?

Cognitive behavior therapy (CBT) has been chosen as a primary approach to teaching ToM in this manual. CBT emphasizes the role of thinking in how we feel and behave. It offers an instructional practice, which empowers the client with knowledge and strategies to render change. The therapist-client relationship is a positive one, where the therapist assumes the role of instructor and promotes active teaching and encouragement. CBT provides a short-term approach to targeting problems and implementing strategies to teach participants to recognize social situations, avoid potential pitfalls, and cope effectively when they encounter challenges.

CBT is backed by empirical support and clinical trials for treating a variety of problems. It provides a structured, goal-directed approach that can be tailored for a variety of children and in an array of treatment settings including individual, small group, and large group (White 2004). There are two critical components of the CBT framework used in this manual: functional analysis and skill training. The core principals of CBT as a general treatment model are outlined here:

- **Functional analysis:** Conducting an analysis of the problem and identifying potential causes for the problem provides critical information, which is necessary to move forward with training. The instructor will help the participants to recognize these problems early in training and to be cognizant of how they affect the self and others throughout learning.

- **Skill training:** Each of the activities in the curriculum targets a specific skill or skill set essential to the development of ToM. The instructor will introduce, model, and provide support to each participant as the concepts are taught. Skills are reviewed after instruction, addressed in multi-sensory activities, and revisited during the following session to reinforce comprehension and generalization. Several methods of teaching are implemented throughout the curriculum to provide skill training, including role playing, cognitive rehearsal, social scripts, and social games.

- **Identification of outcomes:** It is important for participants to recognize the impact that their own behavior may have on another person and how their behavior may alter various situations, thoughts, and feelings for both their partners and themselves. This section of training challenges participants to consider the possible outcomes of their actions, specifically in relation to ToM concepts.

- **Skill application:** This component of training has been added to allow for the instructor to assess the participant's comfort level with the target skill and provide for supplemental instruction or individualized support as needed. This will also encourage generalization of skills outside of these sessions.

- **Encouragement:** This is a critical component to the CBT approach and should be embedded into the teaching methodology and presence of the instructor. Throughout the curriculum, participants will learn to identify with encouragement by giving and accepting compliments to self and others. In later sessions, the reception and delivery of feedback will be introduced as an important stepping-stone in the development of self-assessment and self-regulation skills.

- **Regulation time:** Self-regulation has been identified as a critical skill in early development and may contribute to increased social acceptance. The five-minute "Silly Time" at the end of each session offers the instructor a unique opportunity to observe each participant's ability to self-regulate under conditions of inspired high arousal. In addition, the instructor can teach important strategies such as controlled breathing and response to calming conditions (lights dimmed, instructor's calm counting). These weekly, integrated teachings are designed to enhance the participant's ability to stay calmly focused and alert when necessary, to manage reciprocal social interactions, and to change his/her level of arousal to match a situation.

- **Caregiver letter:** The caregiver letters have been provided to support continued skill enhancement, feedback, and goal adherence outside of the training environment. They offer essential information related to the target skills and core concepts of training. Each caregiver letter contains recommendations for supplemental activities and verbiage to empower family members to address these concepts at home in a non-threatening manner. The content is derived directly from each lesson plan for consistency of information.

IDENTIFYING APPROPRIATE PARTICIPANTS

In order to obtain maximum outcomes from this ToM curriculum, participants should be of a developmental age, which is equivalent to the chronological age wherein children typically develop participatory school skills and are able to demonstrate communication, compliance, basic imitation, and attention to instruction. The activities in this curriculum are best suited for participants who have a minimum chronological age of five. They are not required to be able to read, as dictation may be used as an accommodation for all of the activities.

The assessment of each participant should be conducted prior to acceptance into the 12-week program. Ensuring participant compatibility within the groups will prevent any need for changes after training has begun. Significant behavior disruptions will inhibit the instructor's ability to teach and will impede the outcomes of the program for the entire group. Since there is a pressure on the instructor to cover the objectives of each lesson thoroughly, children who present with maladaptive behaviors or significant attention deficits may benefit from experiencing these teachings in a more intimate and individualized format. A joint session, pairing the child with a sensitivity-trained, typical peer model may produce the best outcomes. However, instructors should carefully assess each participant's readiness for this particular curriculum and take into consideration the compatibility of the child participants when forming a group. My experience leads me to recommend against grouping based solely on diagnosis. The uniqueness of each child's needs and learning styles requires careful planning and grouping to ensure the most beneficial outcomes. Regardless of age or diagnosis, participants should demonstrate delays in the development of social-communication skills.

Instructors will be able to gain insight into appropriate grouping and behavior by having each candidate participate in an informal assessment of conversational skills or via review of a video demonstration of the participant engaged in play with others. This assessment should be conducted prior to acceptance into the program. The information outlined in the next section has been provided to give instructors a deeper understanding of the foundational skills that are common areas of impairment for children who lack ToM. These areas are also highlighted in the pre-post assessment.

PRIOR TO BEGINNING SESSIONS

It is important for the instructor to be prepared prior to the inception of this program. The following preparations should be completed prior to the first session:

- A phone interview is conducted with the caregiver to discuss general concerns and appropriateness for the program. A 20–30 minute screening may be scheduled to allow for the instructor to observe the child in the clinic setting. This may be scheduled with other potential participants if arranged in time. The parent should be notified that video recording will be conducted throughout this program for the purpose of instructor review and measuring outcomes.

- The child visits with the instructor for the screening. The parent will photocopy/download and complete the Parent Social Questionnaire (Appendix C) and Video Consent form (Appendix D) at this time. The instructor may decide to video this session and complete the pre-test portion of the Skill Assessment Scale (Appendix E) if pre-post comparison is desired. The instructor will notify the caregiver that she or he will be contacted regarding program suitability and program start date and time after all of the prospective participants have been screened. It is important for parents to realize that comparable graping is an important element to the success of the program.

- The instructor will continue to screen potential participants, review Parent Questionnaires, and complete the Skill Assessment Scale on appropriate candidates.

- The instructor may want to consider laminating the curriculum materials in this manual for durability. In addition, participants may brainstorm, and ideas or clues can be highlighted directly on to photos, drawings, and activity sheets.

PEER MODELS

When available, peer models can provide an excellent source of modeling age-compatible typical behaviors, social pragmatic language, and paralinguistic cues. Peer models provide a novel dynamic to role plays and allow the adult to act more as a facilitator or coach, rather than a simulated social partner. Peer models may be most beneficial when they:

- are one to two years older than the average age of the group

- can demonstrate appropriate social behavior, maturity, and communication abilities for their chronological age

- have completed sensitivity training related to the exceptionalities of the group participants (also important for siblings of children with special needs)

- recognize their role as participant (peer) models (and not assistant teachers).

It is important to provide peers with some type of sensitivity training prior to using them as peer models. Giving peers an understanding of the challenges children with exceptionalities may face will enhance their interactions, increasing the success of their involvement and empowering them with age-appropriate information. During my sensitivity trainings for typical peer models, I typically review common functions of behavior, strategies for gaining a peer's attention, and patience to increase their responsiveness during participation. I have found peer models to be wonderful catalysts in helping children to reach social goals during treatment sessions. The use of familiar peer models, such as neighbors or siblings, can lend a natural element to training, which may improve the generalization of skills. Novel peers add a less predictable element but enable the child to practice the art of meeting and adapting to new friends. Several good book titles are listed in the Recommended Reading list to support sensitivity training information.

VIDEO ASSESSMENT

The use of video footage is recommended in this series of lessons. It is particularly helpful during activities that focus on the concept of self-assessment. When children observe another person or view a photograph, they have a visual model and can then critique that model based on what they see. Video self-modeling offers this same opportunity, but the child can observe his own behavior and apply self-assessment strategies. Video offers the ability to freeze frame a scene and allow the child to carefully examine and critique his own behavior. In addition, video may serve as a reinforcer, increasing the child's motivation and attention to relevant stimuli (Charlop *et al.* 2010). When a partner is involved in the video, he can dually identify and recognize the behavior of others (Smith-Myles, Trautman, and Schelvan 2004). Video footage may also be used to demonstrate pre-post behaviors, providing children with a chance to compare and discuss their progress following the lessons in this program.

This age group responds well to a "point system" to reinforce the target behaviors during a video review. For example, if the instructor is encouraging the participants to recognize incidents of "matching" behavior during a video, it may help to have each participant mark a + (for matching) or a − (for non-matching) when the video frame is frozen. Participants can add the marks at the end of the video review and use as an incentive, a baseline to compare later video samples, or as a visual to emphasize the frequency of a particular behavior such as "matching." The use of a point system has also led to increased motivation, attention, and behavioral control by the participant during these lessons.

DATA COLLECTION

This program offers a checklist for the instructor to complete for each participant to highlight areas of mastery and discrepancy in the development of target skills. The use of the Skill Assessment Scale allows for the instructor and caregivers to recognize areas where skills are easily mastered, emerging, or in need of continued support. Instructors who are interested in further data collection may explore the false belief task scale developed by Wellman and Liu (2004), who suggest that there is a sequential progression in the development of the concepts of full ToM. These easy-to-administer tests cover a range of beliefs and mental states including the following:

- diverse desires

- diverse belief

- false belief

- knowledge access

- belief emotion

- content false belief

- transfer/location change false belief.

Wimmer and Perner (1983) identified an age trend for the conceptual development of ToM in children between 41–48 months of age. This has been supported by meta-analysis and variations of the false belief tasks (Wellman, Cross and Watson 2001).

The Skill Assessment Scale (Appendix E) offers a list of the concepts as they correlate to the teachings of this 12-week curriculum. The instructor may complete the form to assist caregivers or other professionals in recognizing the participant's areas of strength and weakness following the intensive training. An additional reference, the Target Skill Paradigm (Appendix F), has been provided to guide the instructor with examples of each target skill for the purpose of assessment.

Note: If the instructor chooses to use the Skill Assessment Scale in a pre-post format, it is recommended that an initial, pre-program session should be conducted and video recorded. This informal play session will allow for the instructor to assess each of the skills or review video footage to assess each participant's ability to spontaneously demonstrate the target skills.

SUPPLEMENTAL ACTIVITIES

It is to be anticipated that children who have challenges with ToM will also have delays in the area of reading comprehension, due to their lack of understanding of the very vocabulary which describes mental states in story characters (Antonietti, Liverta-Sempio, and Machetti 2006). An outline of strategies to prevent and overcome comprehension obstacles are highlighted at the end of this manual in a section entitled "Building Comprehension Skills (Appendix A)." It is important to recognize that children who exhibit delays in the areas of development that we will highlight in the next section will likely encounter challenges with reading comprehension. Sophisticated vocabulary, early spelling, and strong decoding skills do not necessarily provide a good prognosis of a child's comprehension abilities. In fact, it is not uncommon for children who have autism to perform well on early tests of decoding, fluency, concrete memory, and the comprehension of the meaning of single words. However, the breakdown becomes visible when higher level elements and complex structures emerge. Children may struggle with the ability to integrate cognitive strategies, such as relating the meaning of text to background information, to interpret the big picture. It is here that the impact of early social deficits manifest in the comprehension of language and reading (Iland 2011).

Although early indicators of reading challenges such as phonemic awareness, receptive language, and difficulty processing auditory information may provide warning signs for later comprehension problems, there are a variety of early indicators that are social in nature and essential to the essence of the early social experience. The absence or delay in development in the areas of imitation, joint attention, language, and pretend play may have a significant impact on later comprehension, as they are critical to the emergence of oral language and vocabulary development (Bergen and Mauer 2000).

CURRICULUM ACTIVITIES

ACTIVITY 1

NAME THAT FEELING

MATERIALS

- Feelings Photo Cards: Unlabeled Sets
- Feelings Photo Cards: Instructor's Labeled Set
- Feelings Word Cards

TARGET SKILL

Participants will learn to identify feelings and label emotions by reading other people's facial expressions or cues.

INSTRUCTIONAL RELEVANCE

During typical development, children watch other people express emotions and learn very early to recognize, read, and represent those emotions. The object of this activity is to enable the participants to identify and label feelings by reading important facial cues found in the eyes, the mouth, and the full face. It is important to place emphasis on the eyes and mouth, as these facial elements are the keys to our expressions. Children who have challenges in reading non-verbal messages will need to develop an ability to recognize cues found in these areas. The instructor should discuss the importance of paying good attention to not only what people say, but to what they do. When we read the gestures, the body language, and the signs and signals, this is called "checking in." It allows us to gain information and watch for "cues." It tells us what people want, how they feel, and even what they are thinking.

The Feelings Photo Cards sets have been designed to display seven specific feelings:

- confused
- excited
- sad
- angry
- bored
- worried
- frustrated.

The Feelings Photo Card deck contains 42 photos. These represent each of the seven feelings in six different people. The people represent both genders and various ages including child, adolescent, and adult. It is important for participants to be able to recognize the same feeling across various subjects to decrease the potential for the participant to develop stereotyped facial expressions for each feeling. The photos also demonstrate the eight emotions as a range of intensity. Whereas many commercial photos depicting feelings will show highly animated renditions of emotion, this Feelings Photo Cards set highlights more subtle changes in facial expressions. The idea is to teach participants to read the "cues" in another's face. The participant's cards are not labeled to allow them to actively focus on these cues, rather than depend on a given label. In addition, a Feelings Photo Cards: Instructor's labeled set is provided for each group of cards. These cards are labeled for group correction.

Children who participate in this program may be challenged with delivering non-verbal information appropriately. This lack of recognition of their own feelings may be a direct result of their lack of observation of other's expressions early in development. The more guided practice they receive in reading the details and "cues," the more connected they will be with various partners. In addition, they will be able to experience what other people are seeing when they express emotions.

ACTIVITIES

1. Feelings Photos and Words Match-up (15 minutes)

Participants should break into pairs of players. Each pair is given one set of Feelings Photo Cards (representing each of the eight target feelings). The partners will work together to examine the faces, read the cues, and match the Feelings Word Cards to the Photo Cards. Instructors may choose to either offer the eight feelings words as choices prior to this activity (i.e. write them on a board or use the Feelings Word Cards provided in this curriculum set) or let participants label them without a prompt. Once the cards are all matched, the instructor will hold up each card in the instructor set for the pairs to check their matches.

Alternate activity: This version will be played with the Feelings Photo Cards only. Have the participants sit in a circle. Two participants will share a set of Feelings Photo Cards. The instructor will choose a card and say the label of the feeling. Each player pair will locate that card in their set and say, "We found (feeling)!" All players will then count down "3, 2, 1" and card holders will lay the target card in the center of the circle simultaneously.

2. How Do I Feel? Game (15 minutes)

The instructor will shuffle the labeled Feelings Photo Cards and give five cards to each player. Each player should hold cards in a fan that only they can see. The remaining cards will be placed faced down in the center of play. The instructor will explain the instructions and model the first turn of play.

The instructor or peer model will model the first turn by turning to the person on the right and saying, "How do I feel?" while demonstrating the expression of a feeling on one of her cards. If the person to the right guesses the feeling correctly, he gets to take all of the cards that show that feeling from the player (i.e. if the player has three sad cards, the partner will take all three for guessing correctly). If he guesses incorrectly, he will draw a card from the pile. Play continues to the right and goes along until one person has all of the cards. If the game does not come to a natural conclusion, players may stop and count their cards. The person with the most cards is the winner.

Note: Some children have a difficult time displaying facial expressions that match their emotion. If a child is challenged in showing a particular feeling, the instructor can point this out when the partner is unable to guess the feeling correctly (and this may happen repeatedly). The instructor can assist the child by modeling the feeling and having her imitate the modeled expression or by looking in a mirror to see what the partner is seeing.

Cognitive Behavioral Concentration

- **Identify outcomes (5 minutes)**
  Discuss the importance of "checking in" when playing or talking with other people. Reference how each participant was "checked in" when guessing what feeling the leader was modeling in the game. Have the group practice "checking in" by giving full attention to the instructor each time he says, "Check in!" Compare the expected response to a "freeze and look" reaction. Allow for each participant to have a turn to call out "Check in" and the instructor will model appropriate eye contact, posture, and quiet listening each time. Consider giving points, checks, or smiley faces on a board for each automatic response. Let the participants know that the term "check in" will be used throughout the sessions to gain attention.

- **Skill application (5 minutes)**
  Ask participants whether they think checking in is easy or difficult to do (looking at faces). Ask them to try to do it more throughout the week.

- **Encouragement (5 minutes)**
  Give compliments to participants for their efforts during the group activities. Avoid generic praise, such as "Good job," and offer descriptive language to highlight skill acquisition, such as, "Henry, you were really checked in during our feelings game. Nice work today!"

- **Regulation time (3–5 minutes)**
  Inform the group that the last five minutes of each session will be reserved for "Silly Play." This provides a good opportunity for the instructor to observe each participant's ability to self-regulate. Engage in one brief activity to bring the group to high arousal. At the end of the activity, the instructor will begin a count down from ten in a clear, calm voice. Inform the participants that "Silly Play" will be offered if they can show that they are capable of bringing their energy level down to a "just right" state before leaving. Have them take one deep breath (in through the nose and out through the mouth) with each number.

Activity: Crab walking under the bridge: Have two people form a bridge with their arms, while the others crab walk under the bridge and around in a circle to go under again and again. Have the "bridge" players choose two players to take their place after one minute is up, and so on until three minutes has passed. The instructor will begin to count down from ten and call on each child as they calm to line up/leave the session.

- **Caregiver letter**
  The instructor will hand out the caregiver letter to provide supplemental information for caregivers to support homework follow-through and generalization of new skills.

ACTIVITY 2

WHAT MAKES ME FEEL...?

MATERIALS

- What Makes Me Feel Worksheet (Appendix G)

- Colored pencils, crayons, or pencils (to act as drawing/writing utensils)

- Small star stickers (in various colors) (optional)

- Balloon

TARGET SKILL

Participants will learn to identify various causes of their emotions and compare/contrast them to their partners.

INSTRUCTIONAL RELEVANCE

The ability to recognize emotional responses is developed early in childhood when children observe the affective reaction of other people to various experiences. The ability to recognize how others feel during social interactions is essential to the success of social cognition, language development, and childhood friendships. As children enter elementary school, it becomes more important to monitor the emotions and behavior of peers to regulate their own behavior to harmonize with a group. However, when a child is not able to sustain attention to social cues such as facial expressions, body language, and gestures, he will unknowingly neglect the hidden social connection. Children with autism are likely to have some level of difficulty expressing their emotions, describing what they are thinking, establishing the cause and effect of their emotions, and in using language related to feelings. Experience and research confirms that children will not learn by observation from a model if they do not attend to the model's behavior. Simply exposing a child to a typical learning environment will not ensure that learning will occur (Bandura 1971).

By 18 months of age, the young child is able to recognize another person's emotion and will offer assistance when another child is in need (Warneken and Tomasello 2006). This behavior develops from social learning that occurs naturally during childhood as a result of the child's careful attention to social cues. This activity will provide controlled reinforcement and direct instruction to assist the participants in connecting external emotional expression to internal feelings in themselves and others.

ACTIVITIES

1. What Makes Me Feel Worksheet (30 minutes)

Participants will sit at a table for this activity. Each participant will have a What Makes Me Feel worksheet and access to writing/drawing utensils. The instructor will have each child place their name in the center. The group should begin with the same feeling and discussion of what makes him feel this emotion. Each child will write words or draw a picture for each thing/person/place that causes the feeling in the appropriate box. Continue until all feelings are completed.

Note: The instructor may allow the child to dictate their answers if they are unable to write.

2. Compare Our Feelings (Time permitting)

The group may remain at the table or sit in a circle on the floor to promote movement. The instructor will give each participant a sheet of stickers (one color per child) and have each child place one sticker of their color at the top of their own worksheet. The first child will say what causes him to feel… If another child identified the same thing on his sheet, he will give a sticker to the speaking child to put next to that feeling. The instructor might model social jargon as a verbal response when giving a sticker to a peer (i.e. "Me too," "So do I," "That's what I wrote"). Ask the next child to say what causes she identified for the next feeling. Repeat with the stickers and continue around the circle until all feelings are discussed. The instructor will point out that the stickers represent the similarities across the group.

Note: This activity can be conducted without the stickers. However, the stickers or other symbols provide an added visual cue to draw the child's attention to the comparison of emotional causes within the group.

Cognitive Behavioral Concentration

- **Identify outcomes (5 minutes)**
  As time allows, ask the question, "What would you do if your friend was feeling…?" The instructor may establish an understanding of the child's ability to respond appropriately to empathy. In addition, correct responses may be reinforced and other options may be modeled for the group.

- **Skill application (5 minutes)**
  Ask participants to learn about the feelings of members of their family. The instructor may conduct a role play of how to initiate questions to gain information about others.

- **Encouragement (5 minutes)**

  Give compliments to participants for their efforts during the group activities. Avoid generic praise, such as "Good job," and offer descriptive language to highlight skill acquisition, such as, "Scott, you really know how to help a friend who is feeling… That was a great answer!"

- **Regulation time (3–5 minutes)**

  Inform the participants that "Silly Play" will be offered if they can show that they are capable of bringing their energy level down to a "just right" state before leaving. Have them take one deep breath (in through the nose and out through the mouth) with each number.

Activity: Balloon lift: Have the participants attempt to prevent a balloon from touching the ground until three minutes has passed. The instructor will begin to count down from ten and call on each child as they calm to line up/leave the session.

- **Caregiver letter**

  The instructor will hand out the caregiver letter to provide supplemental information for caregivers to support homework follow-through and generalization of new skills.

ACTIVITY 3

FOLLOW THE EYES

MATERIALS

- Various small objects
- Follow the Eye Picture Cards
- Dry erase marker (optional)
- Long rope/sheet

TARGET SKILL

Participants will learn to follow another person's gaze to determine what the person is thinking, wanting, or feeling, or intending to do.

INSTRUCTIONAL RELEVANCE

The ability to observe another person intently enough to follow his gaze is a skill that emerges at 10–11 months of age in typical development (Meltzoff and Brooks 2007). It is a prominent first step leading to the child's ability to understand the intentional states of others. Research has indicated that young infants are driven by social cognitive motives. This is the very essence of the child's desire to learn more about people to satisfy their own curiosity (Frith and Frith 2001). The eyes provide a primary source of social information gathering. Following them allows for the child to gain an understanding of others' perceptions and mental states at an early age. Gaze following has also been identified as a predictor of language development (Meltzoff and Brooks 2007).

Children who have been diagnosed with an autism spectrum condition did not likely follow gaze early in development (Leekam, Hunniset, and Moore 1998). This missed milestone may cause significant delays in later social cognition and language development. The two activities in this session will teach the child to acquire information about another person by following eye gaze. Both real partners and pictures are utilized to emphasize that information may be gathered without verbal interaction, gestures, or proximity. Recognizing that another person has perceptual contact with an object will help to answer the child's targeted social questions.

ACTIVITIES

1. Treasure Hunt (20 minutes)

The instructor will hide a small trinket somewhere in the room. Participants will each have a turn to find the location of the hidden object by paying careful attention to the instructor's eye gaze. No verbal or gestural cues should be given. Each player will have a turn to "see" what the instructor "knows."

2. See and Guess (15 minutes)

The instructor will use the Follow the Eye Picture Cards to teach the concept of "eye gaze following" to the participants. Each card shows a line drawing of one or two figures. The instructor will hold one card up and ask the participant(s) the following questions to prompt awareness of mental states:

- "What does he want?" "How do we know this?"

- "What is she thinking?" "How do we know this?"

- "What is he going to do?" "How do we know this?"

Note: If participants demonstrate difficulty following the eye gaze in the picture cards, the instructor should prompt the child to "Place your finger on the eyes and follow their direction to the target." The instructor can also draw a line from the eyes to the target with a dry erase marker.

Cognitive Behavioral Concentration

- **Identify outcomes (5 minutes)**
  As time allows, ask the question, "What am I looking at now?" The instructor will model an eye gaze for the participant to follow. Be sure to look at an obvious object for the first turn. The instructor should gradually increase the level of difficulty by switching the question from looking behavior to mental states (i.e. "What am I thinking about now?").

- **Skill application (5 minutes)**
  Ask participants to play the Treasure Hunt game at home with parents and siblings.

- **Encouragement (5 minutes)**
  Give compliments to participants for their efforts during the group activities. Avoid generic praise, such as "Good job," and offer descriptive language to highlight skill acquisition, such as, "Evan, you did a super job of following the eyes today. What a great detective you are!"

- **Regulation time (3–5 minutes)**
  Inform the participants that "Silly Play" will be offered if they can show that they are capable of bringing their energy level down to a "just right" state before leaving. Have them take one deep breath (in through the nose and out through the mouth) with each number.

Activity: Tug of war: Have the participants sit on opposite ends of a rope or sheet and pull in their direction until three minutes has passed. To add to the silliness, the instructor can encourage each side to choose a "chant" to sound out as they pull (i.e. "Oo-gah!"). The instructor will begin to count down from ten and call on each child as they calm to line up/leave the session.

- **Caregiver letter**
  The instructor will hand out the caregiver letter to provide supplemental information for caregivers to support homework follow-through and generalization of new skills.

ACTIVITY 4

MIRROR MIRROR

MATERIALS

- Two mirrors (not included)
- Music

TARGET SKILL

Participants will learn the importance of imitation as a tool to understand the actions, intentions, and goals of a social partner.

INSTRUCTIONAL RELEVANCE

Studies indicate that children who are diagnosed with autism spectrum conditions exhibit impairment in the spontaneous use of imitation for social gain (Ingersoll 2008). It might be suspected that the deficit in learning through imitation generates from a lack of attention and motivation. Both of these are required to engage in imitation for social learning purposes. Early in development, children imitate a variety of models including actual people, characters as described in stories, and fictional characters who are portrayed in movies and television shows. By 18 months, delayed imitation emerges in the child's play as he incorporates actions that he has previously observed. After 24 months, the child will combine various delayed actions to create play themes from earlier observed actions, such as pretending to prepare a meal for the family or putting the doll in timeout (Eckerman and Stein 1990). Stronger attention to the action of others leads to more intricate imitation that may include specific vocal inflection and mannerisms modeled by familiar people. When the young child is engaging in this type of dramatic play alone, it is evident that his behavior is not influenced by external reinforcement but is self-satisfying. Albert Bandura (1989) described this intrinsic motivation to engage in delayed imitation as *social cognitive theory*. The ability for the child to represent meaningful experiences at a later time influences his understanding of causal relationships, ignites problem-solving abilities, and expands his knowledge of the social world. The imitation of models can also have a profound affect on the child's developing attitudes, beliefs, and emotional disposition.

Imitation plays a crucial role in the connection of cognition, behavior, and environment as a diadic process that mediates learning throughout development (Bandura 1993). Although clinical observation indicates that children who have autism may be able to demonstrate the acquisition of learning imitation through discrete trial instruction, it is important to discriminate between the two primary forms of imitation. Imitation as it pertains to learning might include such skills as functional object manipulation (i.e. use a cup for drinking) and action mimicry (i.e. clap hands in response to a model or jump when given a verbal command). Imitation for social communication would demonstrate the child's ability to take the role of leader and follower, eventually integrating both in a flexible, reciprocal system of responsiveness to a partner. Delays in the social form of imitation may pose a significant disruption in the development of maturing peer relationships through childhood and into adolescence.

The goal of the activities in this session is to encourage interactions that are purely social and spontaneous. Rather than relying on a verbal command to imitate an action, the participant's imitation will be driven by social interest. These types of unpredictable interactions increase the child's attention to non-verbal behaviors and will lead to improved generalization of social imitation skills.

ACTIVITIES

1. Mirror Mirror (15 minutes)

The instructor will ask participants to find a partner. Each pair will get a mirror and sit facing each other. One partner will hold the mirror, look into it and demonstrate a feeling for her partner. The partner will guess how she is feeling. Participants will take turns using the mirror. This activity is particularly helpful for participants who have difficulty expressing their feelings effectively. The mirror offers a visual cue so that they can "check in" with their own facial expressions to determine the effectiveness of their message to the partner.

Note: If participants are exhibiting difficulty with this activity, the instructor may want to use the Feelings Photo Cards (from Activity 1) to provide a visual model of facial expressions.

2. Monkey See, Monkey Do (20 minutes)

This activity will pair the participants and have one child act as the "doer" while the other child is the "mirror." The instructor should model one turn of this game to emphasize that the doer models the first action. The mirror should follow the action each time that the doer changes. Eventually, the mirror should begin to anticipate what the doer will do next.

Note: This activity can be difficult for children who demonstrate a very limited attention span or regulation challenges. In an effort to preserve the lesson, the instructor may want to consider keeping the game in play with only one "doer" for the group.

Cognitive Behavioral Concentration

- **Identify outcomes (5–10 minutes)**
  As time allows, ask the question, "What is different on my face when I change my expression from happy to sad?" The instructor will want to model each of the eight target emotions, demonstrating the similarities and differences. Ask, "Which feelings have eyebrows down?" *Confused, frustrated, and angry.* "Which feelings have eyebrows up?" *Excited, worried, and sad.* Show the participants each of the eyebrow options and change the mouth from turned up to turned down or flat to show six of the eight emotions. After the group is able to recognize these specific cues, demonstrate a bored expression (as a flat mouth and flat eyebrows) and knowing as a mild affect change that send the non-verbal message, "I understand what you are saying" or "I am listening." Have each participant role play each of the eight expressions.

- **Skill application (5 minutes)**
  Ask participants to use the mirror at home to practice making facial expressions.

- **Encouragement (5 minutes)**
  Give compliments to participants for their efforts during the group activities. Avoid generic praise, such as "Good job," and offer descriptive language to highlight skill acquisition, such as, "Taylor, you were a great mirror today. You really paid careful attention to the doer!"

- **Regulation time (3–5 minutes)**
  Inform the participants that "Silly Play" will be offered if they can show that they are capable of bringing their energy level down to a "just right" state before leaving. Have them take one deep breath (in through the nose and out through the mouth) with each number.

Activity: Musical chairs: Have the participants play a game of musical chairs until three minutes has passed. The instructor will begin to count down from ten and call on each child as they calm to line up/leave the session.

- **Caregiver letter**
  The instructor will hand out the caregiver letter to provide supplemental information for caregivers to support homework follow-through and generalization of new skills.

ACTIVITY 5

ALIKE AND DIFFERENT

MATERIALS

- Alike and Different Comparison Sheet (Appendix H)

- Venn Diagram Worksheet (may be laminated for multiple use) (Appendix I)

- Pencil, colored pencils, or markers

- Masking tape

- Straws, one per child

- Pom-poms/cotton balls, one per child

TARGET SKILL

Participants will recognize that other people's desires, thoughts, and opinions may differ from their own.

INSTRUCTIONAL RELEVANCE

Children who have been diagnosed with HFA or AS commonly demonstrate a weakness in the ability to consider that other people's thoughts, beliefs, desires, and knowledge may differ from their own. This inability to appreciate the many different viewpoints of others has been long referred to as "egocentrism." Piaget (1962) discussed evidence of egocentrism in early childhood development. It is marked by a period of time (ages two to seven) wherein the child assumes that everyone thinks as he does, has the same feelings as he does, and wants the same things as he does. It is the child's inability to shift his mental perspective to differentiate his view from another. His thoughts and communications are typically about himself. However, typically after age seven, the child will develop the cognitive resources to make judgments about differing points of view.

By 24 months, a child begins to recognize that others have different likes and dislikes (Repacholi and Gopnik 1997). Some might attribute the systemic social impairment found in autism to this inability to coordinate visual perspectives from an early age. Frith suggests that this naïve egocentrism is exhibited by individuals with AS well into adulthood and across the lifespan, as evidenced in actual accounts from diagnosed individuals. She hypothesizes that the source of their inability to decenter from their own perspective might be a result of weak central coherence (Frith and de Vignemont 2005). This would be supported by clinical observations and caregiver reports indicating that children have difficulty seeing the "big picture" in many life and social situations.

The activities in this lesson will highlight the various points of view that other participants have in relation to one subject. In addition, it will compel the child to consider other people's desires, thoughts, and opinions to compare and contrast them to his own.

ACTIVITIES

1. I Like/You Like/They Like (20 minutes)

The instructor will give each participant an Alike and Different Comparison Sheet (Appendix H) and a writing utensil. The child will place his own name in the first section of the grid, a family member's name in the middle section, and the instructor's name in the last section. The instructor will lead the group through each of the subjects on the left column of the grid. These subjects include various favorites (i.e. movies, foods, people, places). As each subject is addressed, the child will fill in the answer for each name represented at the top of the grid (i.e. self, family member, and instructor). The child should be able to easily answer for himself first. He will then need to make a best guess about the family member's favorite. Finally, he will need to ask the instructor to gain information about his desire in the category. This sequence will continue until all of the sections are filled in. If the child is unable to write, he may draw a picture or dictate answers to the instructor.

Note: Instructors should refrain from correcting participant's initial answers. In many cases, children will place the same answer in all three columns. This would be a reflection of their inability to recognize that the instructor or a family member might have a different point of view about the subject. The instructor should note initial challenges and then model the ability to consider clues that might lead to a correct answer (i.e. things the other person has said about the subject).

2. Venn Diagram (20 minutes)

The instructor will ask the participants to get into pairs and give them a Venn Diagram Worksheet (Appendix I). A subject from the following list will be chosen and written at the top:

- Things I like about the playground

- Things I like about the beach

- About my family

- About me.

Participants will place their names on either the top of the right or left circle of the diagram. The instructor will encourage partners to ask specific questions to each other about the subject and fill in answers on the designated side of the diagram. The instructor may model a variety of questions to promote additional information gathering. The partners will then compare their answers and place any matching answers in the center of the diagram. Continue for additional subjects if time allows.

Cognitive Behavioral Concentration

- **Identify outcomes (5 minutes)**
  As time allows, ask questions to see if participants recall the perspectives of their peers in group such as, "What is…'s favorite movie?" If the participants are able to answer some of these questions, the instructor can alter the language to refer to mental states such as "If… went to the movies, what would she want to watch?" or "If…went to the playground, what would he hope to find there?"

- **Skill application (5 minutes)**
  Ask participants to find out more about their parent's and sibling's likes and dislikes by watching for clues and by asking questions to gain answers. If time allows, the instructor may model some non-verbal clues that would indicate that another person shares the same thoughts or feelings about a subject. For example, each participant in the group would say his favorite (food) and the instructor would display a facial expression of like (smile) or dislike (frown/disgust).

- **Encouragement (5 minutes)**
  Give compliments to participants for their efforts during the group activities. Avoid generic praise, such as "Good job," and offer descriptive language to highlight skill acquisition, such as, "Claire and Kate, you found so many things that you both like. Now you know more about each other!"

- **Regulation time (3–5 minutes)**
  Inform the participants that "Silly Play" will be offered if they can show that they are capable of bringing their energy level down to a "just right" state before leaving. Have them take one deep breath (in through the nose and out through the mouth) with each number.

Activity: Pom-pom races: Place a piece of masking tape down two sides of a table. Each child will have a straw and one pom-pom or cotton ball. On the "Ready, Set, Go," two players will blow the pom-pom across the table with the straw only. Continue to allow for multiple turns until three minutes has passed. To add to the silliness, the instructor can encourage each side to give their partner a "high five" after each turn.

- **Caregiver letter**
The instructor will hand out the caregiver letter to provide supplemental information for caregivers to support homework follow-through and generalization of new skills.

ACTIVITY 6

GOOD GUESSES

MATERIALS

- Riddles Cards Set

- Picture Clues Cards Set

- Instructor Bag containing a variety of items that are suggestive of personal likes, family, etc.

- Questions Prompt Sheet

- Flip chart/Dry erase board (optional)

- Music to be danced to

TARGET SKILL

Participants will learn to use visual and verbal information to make appropriate inferences about a situation or to guess a conclusion.

INSTRUCTIONAL RELEVANCE

The ability to infer has been identified as a predictor of language and reading comprehension. Inference is a skill that allows the child to make reasonable guesses that are based on experiences, previous knowledge, and clues. The clues are in the details of what the child sees (in pictures), knows (from past experiences), and thinks (making connections). Children use inference to make sense of the literary world and their social world. Inference skills play an important role in the development of reading comprehension (Carr, Dewitz, and Patberg 1989). When listening to a story or reading fictional text, the child is required to fill in gaps of information or to "read between the lines." Children base this information on existing schemas or frameworks of acquired information. Reading requires a range of skills that involve the metacognitive process of how one thinks to generate both questions and answers.

Clinical observation indicates that this deficit is evident in two primary areas of development that may pose a challenge in autism: social-language development and reading comprehension. Within both contexts, it is not uncommon for children to understand and answer questions about specific details without understanding the big picture of a story or social scenario (Gately 2008).

Inferencing for the purpose of both social and text connections is made possible when the child is motivated by curiosity and question asking. Relatively any question that is not literal will lead us to making an inference. When a child engages in a process of thought to derive a plausible guess, he is able to answer the question, "How do you know?" The activities in this session provide a fun, interactive way to teach participants to search for important clues, use past experiences, and consider known information to make good, supported guesses.

ACTIVITIES

1. Riddles (15 minutes)

The instructor will use the Riddles Cards Set to stimulate the participant's inference skills. Each card will be read by the instructor with animated character to hold the attention of the group. Riddles offer a motivating learning challenge that ponder several questions, including: What am I? Where am I? and Who am I?

2. Picture Clues (15 minutes)

The instructor will help each participant choose a partner in the group. Each pair will receive one picture from the Picture Clues Cards Set. The instructor will set a sand timer or auditory timer for two minutes and encourage the pairs to look for clues in the picture with their partners. They will find as many clues as possible to answer the instructor's questions about the picture. The three target questions include:

- What happened? (How do you know?)

- How is the person (are the people) feeling? (How do you know?)

- Are there other possibilities? (How do you know?)

Note: The instructor may need to assist in generating answers to the question, "How do you know?" This question is important and should be asked after each of the three target questions to encourage participants to carefully consider all possible clues. The instructor may say, "Let's look at the clues again." It would also be helpful to ask other participants if they "see other clues." Recognition of the clues may alter the reader's opinion.

3. It's In the Bag (15 minutes)

The instructor will have prepared a bag with a variety of items in it that are suggestive of personal likes, family, etc. Each item will serve as a clue for the participants to make guesses about the instructor. The instructor will take each item out of the bag, label it, and place it in the center of the group. Each participant will have an opportunity to make a guess in the form of a question (i.e. "Do you like candy?" upon seeing a box of mints). If a flip chart or dry erase board is available, the instructor may write the guesses for the group to see. Examples of items that might be found in the bag with correlating questions:

• Piece of chocolate	• "Do you like chocolate?"
• Paint brush	• "Do you like to paint?"
• Book	• "Do you like to read?"
• Dog treat	• "Do you have a dog?"
• Gift card to a restaurant	• "Is…your favorite restaurant?"

Use the Questions Prompt Sheet (Appendix J) if participants cannot spontaneously generate questions.

Cognitive Behavioral Concentration

- **Identify outcomes (5 minutes)**
  As time allows, have each participant make a guess about a peer in the group based on something he has said or displays (i.e. "Do you like trucks?" upon seeing a peer's shirt with a truck).

- **Skill application (5 minutes)**
  Ask participants to find out more about their peers at school by making guesses in the form of questions. The instructor may model several examples.

- **Encouragement (5 minutes)**
  Give compliments to participants for their efforts during the group activities. Avoid generic praise, such as "Good job," and offer descriptive language to highlight skill acquisition, such as, "Tory, you were really looking and listening for clues today. Great detective work!"

- **Regulation time (3–5 minutes)**
  Inform the participants that "Silly Play" will be offered if they can show that they are capable of bringing their energy level down to a "just right" state before leaving. Have them take one deep breath (in through the nose and out through the mouth) with each number.

Activity: Dance and freeze: The instructor will play music while the players move and dance around the room, freezing in place every time that the music stops until three minutes has passed. To add to the silliness, the instructor can suggest an animal name when the music stops. The players will move like the animal until the music stops and a new animal name is called.

- **Caregiver letter**
  The instructor will hand out the caregiver letter to provide supplemental information for caregivers to support homework follow-through and generalization of new skills.

ACTIVITY 7

REAL OR PRETEND

MATERIALS

- Various objects (stick, pencil, scarf, block, empty paper towel roll, pebble, envelope, shoelace string) to be kept in a bag/box
- As If Cards Set

TARGET SKILL

Participants will engage in pretend play in the forms of symbolic play and role play for the purpose of social interaction.

INSTRUCTIONAL RELEVANCE

The importance of pretend play in early childhood development has been well documented and marked by well-known theorists of child development, including Piaget, Bandura, and Vygotsky. Pretend play emerges from the child's evolving imitation skills and develops into themes and cooperative role play interactions. The lack of pretend play in the early development of children with autism has been documented since Leo Kanner's early observations in the 1940s (Harris and Jalloul 2012). The absence of pretense may serve as a predictor of later challenges in perspective taking and ToM development. Role play, in particular, allows the child to imagine himself in a specific situation and act "as if" he were someone else. For example, if the child was to pretend to play "schools," he would need to think about how the teacher would act, sound, and interact with the imaginary students. In essence, role play seems to be an important prerequisite to like me/like you thinking and essential in the development of later empathy.

Caregiver reports often indicate that children who have autism seem undermotivated to engage in pretend play. In addition, they lack the desire to engage in pretense as a synchronic unit with another child. They may choose an isolated activity or a more concrete, structured form of play (i.e. puzzles). Wulff (1985) suggests that the weak interpersonal skills that are characteristic of autism may be a result of the child's limited early experiences of sharing and engaging with others in play.

The activities in this lesson will highlight the elements of spontaneity and flexibility as they are typically represented in natural pretend play.

ACTIVITIES

1. What Could It Be? (20 minutes)

The instructor will use the following objects (kept in a bag or box) to stimulate symbolic representation in pretend play:

- stick/pencil
- scarf
- block
- empty paper towel roll
- pebble
- envelope
- shoelace/string.

The instructor will begin by showing the participants one of the objects from the bag/box and saying, "Each one of us will pretend that this object is something else. Let's see how many different ways we can pretend with this." The instructor will model the first turn (i.e. model the use of the stick/pencil as a hammer) and pass the item to the next participant. Each child will contribute a symbolic use of the item until it is passed around the circle. The instructor will pass each item around the group until they are complete.

2. Act As If... (15 minutes)

Each participant will be given a character to act "as if." The instructor will model the first turn by choosing a card from the As If Cards Set. Each participant will choose a different card until they have all been acted out.

Note: Participants may need prompts to consider what the character would act like, sound like, look like, etc.

Cognitive Behavioral Concentration

- **Identify outcomes (5 minutes)**
  As time allows, place the symbolic objects in the center of the group and ask if anyone has a pretend idea for combining two of the objects—for example, using the stick and the string to pretend to eat spaghetti with a fork.

- **Skill application (5 minutes)**
  Ask participants to play "What Could It Be?" at home with caregivers or siblings.

- **Encouragement (5 minutes)**
  Give compliments to participants for their efforts during the group activities. Avoid generic praise, such as "Good job," and offer descriptive language to highlight skill acquisition, such as, "Gabe, you had us believe that you were a pilot! That was super pretending!"

- **Regulation time (3–5 minutes)**
  Inform the participants that "Silly Play" will be offered if they can show that they are capable of bringing their energy level down to a "just right" state before leaving. Have them take one deep breath (in through the nose and out through the mouth) with each number.

Activity: Duck, duck, goose: The instructor will engage the group in Duck, duck, goose until three minutes has passed. To add to the silliness, the instructor can replace the words "duck" and "goose" with other animal names (e.g. "frog" and "snake").

- **Caregiver letter**
  The instructor will hand out the caregiver letter to provide supplemental information for caregivers to support homework follow-through and generalization of new skills.

ACTIVITY 8

QUESTION WEBS

MATERIALS

- Question Web Worksheet (Appendix K)

- Pencils, colored pencils, or markers

- Flip chart/Dry erase board (optional)

- Two cups per pair

- Ping-pong ball/Cotton ball per pair

TARGET SKILL

Participants will identify questions that are appropriate for social interactions and recognize the role of self-initiation in gaining social information about another person.

INSTRUCTIONAL RELEVANCE

The research of Robert and Lynn Koegel emphasizes the critical role of self-initiated queries in the development of language and social pragmatics (Koegel, Carter, and Koegel 2003). They identified self initiations as one of the primary target skills in their Pivotal Response Treatment approach. Their contribution to the practice of child-directed training is invaluable. Question-asking behavior is commonly lacking in children who have autism and, yet, it is essential to the success of a social conversation. Clinical observation indicates that children may be limited in their ability to engage in a reciprocal conversation. Their communication is likely marked by one-sided statements, echoic initiations, or response to direct questions from a partner. Due to the highly structured and rote instruction of many treatments, children may be taught to initiate a conversation by saying, "Hello, my name is..." Although this is an appropriate introduction in some formal social situations, it is not all too common on the playground or at the lunchroom table. In addition, caregivers often report that the child may initiate the first statement and then "get stuck."

Early in child development, question-asking behavior serves multiple purposes. Questions open the door to learning, enhance expressive language, and satisfy the child's inner curiosities about the world. Answers to questions are stored in the child's memory and help to build those schemas that are necessary to help the child to organize and perceive new information.

The activities in this session will teach participants to think flexibly when initiating a partner to gain information by considering many possible queries related to a given topic or situation.

ACTIVITIES

1. Question Webs (20 minutes)

The instructor will use the Question Web Worksheet (Appendix K) to encourage participants to brainstorm questions that would be appropriate for a specific topic or condition. The instructor will label the center of the web with one of the topics or situations listed here and write the participant's questions in the spaces surrounding the web:

- Coloring next to another child

- At the lunch table

- On the playground

- A classmate has fallen down

- Someone is playing with your favorite toy

- You have the same book as another child.

Note: If a flip chart or dry erase board is available, the Question Web may be conducted on a larger surface to enhance visual attention.

2. Real Questions (15 minutes)

The instructor will ask a main question to the group to prompt a topic. Participants will raise their hand if the topic question pertains to them (i.e. if they like pizza, they will raise a hand). The instructor will call on a participant who will initiate a topic-related question to one of the participants who raised a hand (i.e. "Do you like pepperoni on your pizza?"). Here are suggestions for the instructor prompts:

- "Who likes pizza?"

- "Who likes to swing?"

- "Who likes to watch TV?"

- "Who does not like balloons?"

- "Who does not like rollercoasters?"

- "Who has a favorite book?"

- "Who likes ice cream?"

Cognitive Behavioral Concentration

- **Identify outcomes (5 minutes)**
  As time allows, have each participant initiate one question to the instructor to learn something new. Remind the group to refrain from asking a question if they already know the answer.

- **Skill application (5 minutes)**
  Ask participants to choose a topic for mealtime to have family members play the Question Web game.

- **Encouragement (5 minutes)**
  Give compliments to participants for their efforts during the group activities. Avoid generic praise, such as "Good job," and offer descriptive language to highlight skill acquisition, such as, "Kyle, your questions are really helping you to get to know everyone here. Well done!"

- **Regulation time (3–5 minutes)**
  Inform the participants that "Silly Play" will be offered if they can show that they are capable of bringing their energy level down to a "just right" state before leaving. Have them take one deep breath (in through the nose and out through the mouth) with each number.

Activity: Ping-pong ball catch: The instructor will give each pair two cups and a ping-pong ball (or cotton ball). Partners will "throw" the ball with the cup to the partner's cup in a reciprocal game until three minutes has passed. To add to the silliness, the instructor can encourage one partner to say "ping" when the ball is tossed and the other "pong" when attempting to catch the ball.

- **Caregiver letter**
  The instructor will hand out the caregiver letter to provide supplemental information for caregivers to support homework follow-through and generalization of new skills.

ACTIVITY 9

CHATTER LADDER

MATERIALS

- Chatter Ladder Worksheet (Appendix L)

- Pencils, colored pencils, or markers

- Beach ball

- Dry erase marker

- Bubble wrap/Bubble maker

- Flip chart/Dry erase board (optional)

TARGET SKILL

Participants will identify initiations and responses that are appropriate for reciprocal conversations.

INSTRUCTIONAL RELEVANCE

Once a child receives a response to a social question, she will likely be encouraged to ask another question, add a comment, or share an emotion with her partner(s). This reciprocal exchange of verbal and non-verbal information constitutes a conversation. Clinical observations suggest that children with autism exhibit impairment in the behaviors required to engage in successful conversations. In many cases, their communication is reserved for self-fulfilling purposes, such as making requests and self-stimulatory speech (i.e. perseveration, echolalia).

Studies by Charlop-Christy and colleagues (Charlop and Milstein 1989; Charlop *et al.* 2010) have indicated that appropriate training can lead to the acquisition of conversational skills such as turn taking, enhanced understanding of mental states, novel response substitution, and non-verbal intentions. Her research on the use of video modeling has greatly enriched the existing collection of treatment methods and will be reviewed in later activities. In addition, Carol Gray has contributed to the development of conversational skills with her *Comic Strip Conversations* (1994). In this approach, drawing and symbolic color coding are used as tools to provide enhanced visual support to children with autism. Attention is called to the important features of conversations such as turn taking, perspective taking, and language pragmatics.

These activities will teach participants to think flexibly when engaging in conversations by considering many possible queries, responses, and shifts related to a given topic. Typical peer models add novelty and simulate strong attention skills during these reciprocal activities.

ACTIVITIES

1. Chatter Ladder (20 minutes)

The instructor will use the Chatter Ladder Worksheet (Appendix L) to encourage participants to brainstorm questions and responses that would be appropriate for a specific topic. The instructor will label the top of the ladder with one of the topics listed here and write the participant's questions, comments, and responses on the rungs of the ladder. Examples have been provided for the first two topics and should be recorded as they are spoken during this activity.

- Movies
  I saw… Have you seen…?
  I liked that movie. Do you like…?
  Me, too. What is your favorite movie?
  I did not see… Did you go to the theater?
  I have that movie at home.

- Sports
  I like to play… Do you play…?
  …is fun. What do you play?
  I have played goalie before. Where do you play…?
  I do not like… I like… Who is your coach?

- Computer Games

- Favorite Foods

- Pets

- Riding on an Airplane.

The instructor will remind participants to stay on topic and may consider writing off-topic responses on a separate sheet of paper titled "Off-topic." This can provide a visual prompt and encourage error-correction.

Note: If a flip chart or dry erase board is available, the Question Web may be conducted on a larger surface to enhance visual attention.

2. Keep It In Play (15 minutes)

The instructor will ask a participant to choose a topic. The topic will be written on a beach ball with a dry erase marker. The instructor will initiate the first topic-related question or comment and pass the ball to another player, who will respond to the initiation and pass the ball to another player. The instructor will remind participants to remain "checked in" in case they are given the ball. This will encourage sustained attention, as this behavior is required during conversations.

Note: If the participants are exhibiting difficulty with attention during this game, the instructor can model the initiation by calling the recipient's name first (i.e. "Jacob, do you like…?"). The name may provide an additional, auditory cue that is necessary early in the teaching of these skills.

Cognitive Behavioral Concentration

- **Identify outcomes (5 minutes)**
  As time allows, have each participant engage in a brief, two-way conversation with the instructor or peer model. Introduce a topic that was not previously covered. A good topic might be "What will you do when you leave this group?" Responses may reflect plans such as homework, playing, going on a computer, reading, having dinner or taking a bath.

- **Skill application (5 minutes)**
  Ask participants to choose a topic for mealtime to have family members play the Chatter Ladder game. Participants will be notified to bring a stuffed animal or toy from their room for the next session.

- **Encouragement (5 minutes)**
  Give compliments to participants for their efforts during the group activities. Avoid generic praise, such as "Good job," and offer descriptive language to highlight skill acquisition, such as, "Janet, I noticed that you had a lot of things to add to our Chatter Ladders today. Excellent way to keep the group talking!"

- **Regulation time (3–5 minutes)**
  Inform the participants that "Silly Play" will be offered if they can show that they are capable of bringing their energy level down to a "just right" state before leaving. Have them take one deep breath (in through the nose and out through the mouth) with each number.

Activity: Bubble wrap stomp: The instructor will spread bubble wrap out on the floor. Participants will stomp on the bubble wrap until three minutes has passed. To add to the silliness, the instructor can encourage one partner to say "bam" each time they stomp. If bubble wrap is not available, bubbles make for a fun stomping replacement, too.

- **Caregiver letter**
  The instructor will hand out the caregiver letter to provide supplemental information for caregivers to support homework follow-through and generalization of new skills.

ACTIVITY 10

POINT OF VIEW

MATERIALS

- Paper for drawing

- Pencils, colored pencils, or markers

- Point of View Prompt Cards

- Stuffed animal or toy (brought with participant to class)

- Two different cereal boxes

- Cup

- An apple

- A block

TARGET SKILL

Participants will be taught to consider the perspective of a person or character, as it may differ from their own.

INSTRUCTIONAL RELEVANCE

During early development, a child is experiencing an enormous growth in his social awareness. By age four, the child is beginning to gain an understanding of his own feelings, ways to express emotions, ways to respond to emotions, and causes of his own feelings and the feelings of others. Social perception involves the integration of various skills. These mechanisms allow for the child to monitor imitation and perspective taking skills to maintain like me/like you thinking:

- sustained attention

- behavioral regulation

- consideration of self/other thoughts

- shifting.

For the purpose of laying a basic foundation of perspective taking, two forms of this skill are considered here. Visual perspective taking occurs when the child recognizes that another person has a different line of sight of an object. This perceptual level thinking refers to what the child can "see" versus what the other person can "see" from different points of view (sight). Social perspective taking occurs when the child recognizes that his own mental states differ from another person's.

This conceptual level thinking refers to what the child "thinks, knows, believes" versus what another person "thinks, knows, believes" about the same thing (Yue, Su, and Chan 2011).

Perspective taking relies on the executive functions of the brain and cognitive flexibility. It warrants both ability and motivation. Considering that these skills are commonly considered areas of significant weakness in children who have autism, attention to them should be met with the same vigor with which we emphasize reading, writing, and math.

The activities in this session are designed to target several areas of perceptual (visual) and conceptual (social) perspective taking, as they teach the child to differentiate her point of view from another person's or character's point of view.

ACTIVITIES

1. I See and You See (25 minutes)

Prior to this activity, the instructor will set out three objects in each of two displays in the center of the table as follows:

Display 1

A cereal box will stand in the center with the front side facing one of the chairs and the back side facing the other chair. A cup will be placed directly in front of the cereal box and an apple will be placed directly behind the cereal box.

Display 2

A different cereal box will stand in the center with the front side facing one of the chairs and the back side facing the other chair. A crayon will be placed directly in front of the cereal box and a block will be placed directly behind the cereal box.

The instructor will pair the participants. The pairs should sit directly across from one another at the table with one of the displays in between each pair. The instructor will give each child a piece of paper and drawing utensil(s) and instruct each child to "Draw what your partner sees."

When the drawings are complete, invite the participants to sit in a circle on the floor to share their drawings. Have each child take his drawing to his partner's chair, sit in that chair, and compare his drawing with the actual display as it was perceived by the partner from the other side. Participants may draw a circle around items in their drawing that were accurate and draw an "X" on items that were not seen by the partner.

Note: Children who have not formed a basic concept of perspective taking will not likely adjust their behavior to accommodate their partner's point of view (i.e. peek around the cereal box, move to the other side). The instructor should make a note of this and emphasize this concept again in later sessions.

2. The Life of a Rock (20 minutes)

The instructor will use the Point of View Prompt Cards to encourage participants to generate thoughts from the perspective of a character or inanimate object. The instructor will model the first picture card (the rock inside of a cup) by placing it in the center of the group and saying, "Let's think about what it is like to be this rock." The instructor will model various comments related to the mental states of this characterized object. The following mental state vocabulary should be modeled:

- Think
- Hope
- Want
- Feel

- Know
- Wish
- Believe
- Remember

The instructor will speak "as if" she is the rock. Examples of commentary might include:

- "I want to get out of this cup."
- "I feel so lonely in here."
- "I wish I had a friend."
- "I hope someone doesn't drink me."
- "I think I can jump!"
- "I know I can jump!"
- "I just remembered… I can't jump!"
- "Now, I feel sad."

Some of the cards will show two characters. The instructor may assign two players to represent each character. In some pictures, accurate perspective taking will involve a relationship between the two characters. For example, in the picture of the girl and the piece of cake, the girl is obviously thinking about the cake and the cake might be fearful of being eaten by the girl. Continue play until all of the picture cards have been completed.

The Point of View Picture Cards are purposefully ambiguous to encourage the child to consider a variety of possibilities. Cards that depict people do not indicate obvious emotions, while other cards use non-living objects as "characters." This allows the child to use previous information to make a guess in an attempt to interpret the situation. The instructor may reinforce and challenge diverse comments from participants. Each child in the group may extract different details as clues that lead to an assortment of viewpoints. Use the "think aloud" technique to model possibilities and generate "What if" questions.

Note: If participants are having difficulty seeing a character's point of view, encourage them to "Ask a friend in the group for ideas" or "Brainstorm with a partner."

3. What It's Like to Be Me (10 minutes)

Have each participant bring their stuffed animal or toy from home to the circle. Each child will hold their item and talk for one to two minutes about what it is like to live in the participant's room. The instructor will encourage each child to speak "as if" they are the item.

Cognitive Behavioral Concentration

- **Identify outcomes (5 minutes)**
  As time allows, ask participants if they thought that it was easy or difficult to "see" what their partner was "seeing" in the first activity. What strategies did they use to adjust their perspectives? (i.e. peek around the cereal box, move to the other side.)

- **Encouragement (5 minutes)**
  Give compliments to participants for their efforts during the group activities. Avoid generic praise, such as "Good job," and offer descriptive language to highlight skill acquisition, such as, "Chris, you did a nice job of talking for your toy. You really know what it is thinking!"

- **Regulation time (3–5 minutes)**
  Inform the participants that "Silly Play" will be skipped during this session due to the length of the activities.

- **Caregiver letter**
  The instructor will hand out the caregiver letter to provide supplemental information for caregivers to support homework follow-through and generalization of new skills.

ACTIVITY 11

ME VS WE

MATERIALS

- Me vs We Cards

- Various toys (representing a mix of concrete and abstract; suitable for individual/pairs play)

- Play theme set

- Video camera

TARGET SKILL

Participants will identify the importance of "we" play vs "me" play in photos and real-life situations.

INSTRUCTIONAL RELEVANCE

Cooperative play is an essential stage of child development wherein important life skills are learned. When children are playing together, they are working, planning, sharing, taking on roles, engaging creativity, problem-solving, and developing relationships. Cooperative play enhances language development and teaches children about cultural society. Together, children ignite big-picture thinking.

Pamela Wolfberg's studies involving her Integrated Play Group (IPG) model provides inspiring outcomes to support the use of peer models in promoting cooperative play in children with autism (Wolfberg, Bottema-Beutel, and DeWitt 2012; Wolfberg and Schuler 1993). Clinical observations have demonstrated increases in social play, language, and in the generalization of learned skills when the IPG approach was implemented. Instructors are encouraged to review the literature of this program to enhance treatment outcomes with this target population.

ACTIVITIES

1. Is it Me or Is it We? (15 minutes)

The instructor will use the Me vs We Photo Cards to teach participants to discriminate between "me" play and "we" play. Cards may be sorted into two piles (Me/We) for visual representation. The instructor should ask the question, "How do you know?" to encourage participants to identify the clues in each picture. Some examples of clues:

Me Play	We Play
Child is playing alone.	Children are playing together.
Child is not sharing toys.	Children are sharing the toys.
Child is not "checked in."	Child is looking at others.
Child is turned away.	Child is helping another child.
Child does not notice how the others feel.	Children are laughing together.

We Play in Free Play (20 minutes)

The instructor will tell the children that they will have "We" play time and the toys will change when the time is up. For the first video period (eight minutes), the instructor will offer one dramatic play set for the group. This should be something that can be used for cooperative, pretend play by the group. Here are some suggestions:

- dollhouse

- play food and cooking set

- play tool set with vehicles

- trains with tracks

- blocks with animals

- dress-up clothes.

When the time is up, the group will clean the toys up. For the next video period (eight minutes), the instructor will offer a bucket with a variety of toys for choice. These should be toys that can be played with in isolation or with a partner and represent a mix of concrete and abstract toys. Here are some suggestions:

- a puzzle

- cars and trucks

- a doll with doctor kit

- a squish ball

- a bowling set

- small toy figures (characters).

Cognitive Behavioral Concentration

- **Identify outcomes (5 minutes)**
  As time allows, ask the participants to rate their play by giving themselves a thumbs-up if they engaged in "We" play, a thumbs down if they engaged in "Me" play, and a thumb in the middle if they are unsure.

- **Skill application (5 minutes)**
  Ask participants to practice "We" play more at home and school. Let them know that they will watch a video of their free play in the next session.

- **Encouragement (5 minutes)**
  Give compliments to participants for their efforts during the group activities. Avoid generic praise, such as "Good job," and offer descriptive language to highlight skill acquisition, such as, "Dylan, your 'We' play made your partners feel good today!"

- **Regulation time (3–5 minutes)**
  Inform the participants that "Silly Play" will be offered if they can show that they are capable of bringing their energy level down to a "just right" state before leaving. Have them take one deep breath (in through the nose and out through the mouth) with each number.

Activity: I went walking...: The instructor will tell a story that involves various movements. Participants will listen to the story and imitate the instructor's movements until three minutes has passed. The instructor should incorporate suspense and animation to hold the group's attention. A sample story might sound/look like this:

One day, I took out my backpack [pretends to pick up a bag] and filled it with snacks, binoculars, and a jacket [pretends to place each item in the bag]... I put my hat on [pretends to put hat on head]...

Then, I opened the door [pretends to turn the knob and open the door to go out] and went walking [stands up and walks in place]…

I went into the woods…it was dark and scary [makes a scared expression while walking in place]…

I took my binoculars out of my backpack [pretends to take item out] and looked through them [holds pretend binoculars up to eyes]…

Then, I saw…a BEAR! [makes scared face]… I jumped [jumps in place] and threw my binoculars into the woods [pretends to toss binoculars]…

I ran home as fast as I could [runs in place]…

I opened the door [pretends to turn the knob and go inside]…ran up the stairs [runs with knees up in place]…went into my bed [lies on floor]…

I pulled the covers over my head [pretends to cover self with blanket]…

Whew, that was close! [wipes brow and shows expression of relief]

- **Caregiver letter**
  The instructor will hand out the caregiver letter to provide supplemental information for caregivers to support homework follow-through and generalization of new skills. This letter will remind caregivers that the next session will be the last.

ACTIVITY 12

SELF-ASSESSMENT

MATERIALS

- Video samples
- Self-assessment Worksheet

TARGET SKILL

Participants will engage in self-assessment and problem-solving strategies.

INSTRUCTIONAL RELEVANCE

Perhaps one of the most powerful methods of analyzing one's own behavior is to be able to see oneself in action. Children who have social challenges are not likely to have many opportunities to actually observe themselves as they interact with others. These opportunities allow for the participants to engage in self-critique and effective assessment, which leads to problem-solving and self-correction of behavior. Experience suggests that any child will be less likely to alter their own behavior based on being repeatedly told to do so by an adult. In fact, frequent verbal reminders may very well become ignored by the child after a period of time and the words rendered meaningless.

Research continues to build on the effective outcomes of video self-modeling, which has been identified as an effective strategy to teach perspective-taking in children with autism spectrum disorder (Charlop-Christy and Daneshvar 2003). Video self-modeling is an effective strategy for allowing children to engage in active observation and assessment of their own behaviors. The opportunity to be able to "freeze-frame" these visual demonstrations for examination and discussion is an ancillary benefit. Consistent practice with video self-assessment may lead to an increase in the participants' regulation of verbal and non-verbal communication skills such as facial expressions, gestures, and intonations (Charlop *et al.* 2010).

ACTIVITIES

1. Video Review (30 minutes)

The instructor will give each participant a Self-Assessment Worksheet (Appendix M) and a writing utensil. Participants will view the video samples. The instructor will pause or stop the video at various points to allow the participants to critique their social performance by placing a + or – next to each target skill. The instructor will review each target skill aloud when the video is paused by asking:

- "Are you checked in with your eyes?" (Child will make a + or – next to this skill.)

- "Are you checked in with your body?" (Child will make a + or – next to this skill.)

- "Are you in 'We' play?" (Child will make a + or – next to this skill.)

When the video is completed, the instructor will encourage discussion and compliments amongst peers in the group for skills in which they have noticed improvement in each other.

Program Review

Instructors should take some time to review each of the post-test items with the participants and complete the pre-post test form to send home with the final caregiver letter. The instructor should mark a + or – to indicate the child's ability to demonstrate knowledge of each skill. A description of knowledge criteria is provided on the form.

Cognitive Behavioral Concentration

- **Identify outcomes (5 minutes)**
  As time allows, the instructor may encourage participants to use the + and − marks on their Self-Assessment worksheets to help them to set goals for "We" play. Ideas for goals setting may be modeled.

- **Skill application (5 minutes)**
  Ask participants to watch more video samples of their play and skills outside of the sessions to help them to reach their goals.

- **Encouragement (5 minutes)**
  The instructor should give one overall compliment to each participant about his or her growth during the sessions. The instructor could offer certificates to each participant for their outstanding progress.

- **Caregiver letter**
  The instructor will hand out the caregiver letter to provide supplemental information for caregivers to support homework follow-through and generalization of new skills. The list of recommended readings should be sent with caregivers to provide additional resources to extend ToM development following this 12-week program.

APPENDIX A

BUILDING COMPREHENSION SKILLS

BUILDING COMPREHENSION SKILLS

Reading without comprehension is reading without meaning. Many children may be able to perform well in decoding and fluency, but when asked to discuss what they have read, they are unable to respond. After kindergarten, children are expected to read more complex text leading to paragraph reading and chapter books in the second grade. Children who exhibit impaired ToM may also experience challenges in comprehending narrative reading selections despite their ability to outshine their peers in early reading skills. Children who present with precocious reading or word-recognition skills at an early age are identified as having "hyperlexia." Though initially impressive, this scenario is often accompanied by a significant discrepancy in decoding and comprehension (Randi, Newman, and Brigovenko 2010). When we consider the skills that are essential in the success of social pragmatic language and reading comprehension, the correlation with ToM becomes evident. Like social interaction, reading comprehension involves a wide range of cognitive abilities. Both areas of development require the ability to read social (contextual) clues and print (text) clues. Fiction reading focuses on the ability to identify the plot, setting, character development, vocabulary, figurative language, themes, and conflict. Like social interactions, characters in fiction engage with each other in dynamic ways. The reader is expected to understand vocabulary related to the character's mental states to draw conclusions in narrative text. Descriptive vocabulary can provide a keen reader with imagery clues to understand, visualize, and discuss the intricate weave of storytelling. It is similar to the pretense that was referred to earlier in this manual as a significant impairment in the development of many children who have social challenges.

We can anticipate that impairments in early social language development may be an indication of later challenges in inferential reading comprehension. Our suspicion may be enhanced when the child also exhibits weak phonemic awareness. Failure to address these struggles will result in a widening gap in reading skills. Early, direct instruction in reading comprehension may teach monitoring and repair strategies, while focusing on the cognitive processes that will enhance reading for meaning. The following difficulties may be identified:

- restricted meaning for words despite verbal repertoire

- figurative language (imagery, idioms, metaphors, similes, irony)

- grasping the main idea

- drawing conclusions

- making inferences from conversation or text

- recognizing characters' unique thoughts, ideas, and feelings

- interpreting characters' perspectives

- understanding characters' motives.

Intervention in reading comprehension can accompany the curriculum in this manual, or be addressed as a follow-up in the clinic. First through to third grade participants have responded very well to the direct instruction of strategies to enhance reading with meaning. Chapter books are selected based on their ability to tell stories of colorful characters and imaginary adventures. Each story is presented as a read-aloud and initially read by the instructor. A flip chart is used to model the use of target strategies to enhance the child's understanding as the story unfolds.

The image below shows an example of a chart page used with an eight-year-old child for a chapter of *Charlotte's Web*.

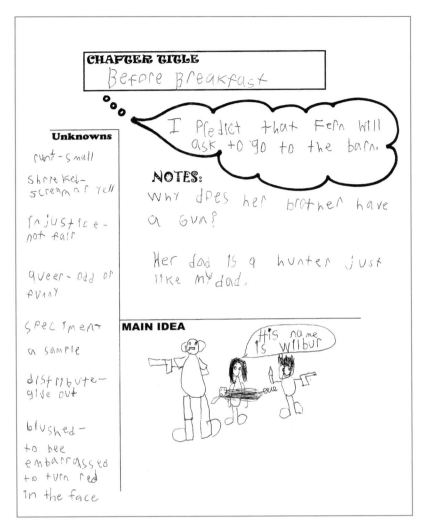

The following strategies are modeled and applied to each story on chart paper:

- **Curiosity and clues:** First, we call the child's attention to the title of the story and the cover. We consider the words and pictures as clues to help us to make a prediction about what we will uncover in the story. The child is prompted to ask as many questions as possible about this story.

- **Make predictions:** Next, we turn to the first chapter and look for clues in the chapter title. A guess bubble is drawn under the title and the child makes a prediction about what will be discovered in the next pages.

- **Flag unknowns:** Teach the child to hold up a hand or say "Stop!" when he hears a word that is unfamiliar. Initially, the instructor may need to prompt the child to identify words that are unknown. These words are written on the chart with a definition or synonym and may be acted out to offer kinesthetic input to promote learning. The instructor may reread the sentence with a synonym in place of the word to enhance meaning.

- **Read and stop:** The instructor should stop reading after transitional sentences and at the end of each page to generate questions about what will happen next.

- **Retell and summarize:** At the end of each chapter, the instructor may help the child to summarize key details and reword the events. The child should be encouraged to sequence the events in the order they occurred in the chapter. Questions that answer who, what, where, and why will spark the child's memory.

- **Visualize:** Using available illustrations and clues found in descriptive vocabulary, the child will think about the text and create mental images of what has happened in the story.

- **Infer:** The child is encouraged to use the knowledge and information she has generated from clues to draw conclusions. Inferencing is often referred to as reading "between the lines" because information is not concretely stated, but rather implied.

- **Identify main idea:** To help the child to see the big picture, the instructor will ask him to identify the main idea of the chapter. This helps the child to sequence information into a hierarchy of importance and pull all of the details together.

- **Draw:** The child will draw a picture of the main idea and key clues on the chart. This will serve as a visual reminder during chapter by chapter recall throughout the book.

- **Make text to self, text to world, text to text connections:** The child will learn to use personal experiences to make sense of the text and to make meaningful connections to characters and situations. Statements like, "This reminds me of…", "That happened to me…", or "This is like my family" can significantly enhance the child's ability to understand the story.

This sequence of strategy use is repeated for each chapter and then the book as a whole. Children who exhibit significant impairments in language and reading comprehension may benefit from multiple sessions per week until strategy use becomes more spontaneous and progress is noted. The use of chart paper is important, as pages may be posted in sequence and saved for later recall. It also provides a nice visual brainstorming surface.

Chapter book series are excellent for practicing these strategies, as they allow the child to get to know the characters in a variety of situations and adventures. Here are a few good examples:

- *The Magic Tree House* series by Mary Pope Osborne

- *The A to Z Mysteries* by Ron Roy

- *Charlotte's Web* by E.B. White

- *The Buddy Files* by Dori Hillestad Butler

- *Ivy and Bean* series by Annie Barrows

- *Ready Freddy* series by Abby Klein

- *My Father's Dragon* by Ruth Stiles Gannett

- *Flat Stanley* books by Sara Pennypacker

- *The Mercy Watson* series by Kate Dicamillo.

APPENDIX B

CAREGIVER LETTERS

FEELINGS AND EXPRESSIONS: A REVIEW OF VOCABULARY

During typical development, children watch other people express emotions and learn very early to recognize, read, and represent those emotions. The object of this activity is to allow the participants to identify and label feelings by reading important facial cues found in the eyes, the mouth, and the full face. It is important to place emphasis on the eyes and mouth, as these facial elements are the key to our expressions. Children who have challenges in reading non-verbal messages will need to develop an ability to recognize cues found in these areas.

The Feelings Photo Card Sets have been designed to display seven specific feelings: confused, excited, sad, angry, bored, worried, and frustrated. Today, your child has rehearsed emotion identification and expression. The more guided practice she or he receives in reading the details and "cues," the more connected they will be with various social partners. In addition your child will be able to experience what other people are seeing when they express emotions.

Here are a few extension activities to enhance your child's generalization of these concepts at home:

- Set up a game show format for guessing each person's feelings by reading facial "cues."

- Use feelings vocabulary throughout the week, emphasizing the seven feelings that were reviewed in this session. Comment on your child's feelings, "I can tell that you are feeling… because your eyes look…" Be sure to call attention to the "cues" that suggest a particular feeling so that your child can recognize the changes in expressions more easily. Also, let your child know when his or her facial expressions do not match their feeling.

- Play "Simon Says" in a mirror with both partners watching for changes in expression in the reflection.

- Be careful not to make a "game" out of your child's moments of intense feelings. This may only lead to confusion. Wait until a later time to engage in a teachable moment focused on feelings vocabulary.

FEELINGS CAUSE AND EFFECT

The ability to recognize emotional responses is developed early in childhood when children observe the affective reaction of other people to various experiences. The ability to recognize how others feel during social interactions is essential to the success of social cognition, language development, and childhood friendships. As children enter elementary school, it becomes more important to monitor the emotions and behavior of peers to regulate their own behavior in order to harmonize with a group. However, when a child is not able to sustain attention to social cues such as facial expressions, body language, and gestures, she or he will unknowingly neglect the hidden social connection. This behavior develops from social learning that occurs naturally during childhood as a result of the child's careful attention to social cues.

Today's activities provided your child with controlled reinforcement and direct instruction to assist them in connecting external emotional expressions (what the face shows) to internal feelings (what caused us to feel this way) in themselves and others. In addition, we compared and contrasted the differences in people's emotional reactions to the same event. This lays an important social foundation in encouraging your child to engage in "like me"/"like you" thinking. You can help to foster your child's understanding that we all may have different thoughts, feelings, and reactions. This skill helps to break egocentric thinking and prompts the emergence of perspective taking.

You can support the development of these skills at home with the following activities:

- Encourage a mealtime conversation about each family member's day. Emphasize events that made each person feel happy, sad, surprised, worried, frustrated, etc.

- Use teachable moments to point out other people's extreme emotions, such as excitement and anger. Help your child to make a connection and express the potential causes for the emotion. If a definite answer is not available, help your child to search for clues to make a guess.

THE IMPORTANCE OF EYE GAZE DETECTION

The ability to observe another person intently enough to follow his gaze is a skill that emerges within the first year of typical development. It is a prominent first step leading to the child's ability to understand the intentional states of others. Research has indicated that young infants are driven by social cognitive motives. This is the very essence of the child's desire to learn more about people to satisfy their own curiosity. The eyes provide a gateway into social information gathering. In addition, gaze following has also been identified as a strong predictor of language development.

Children who have social-communication delays may not have developed an ability to follow gaze early in development. This missed milestone may cause significant delays in later social cognition and language development.

The two activities in today's session were chosen to teach your child how to acquire information about another person by following eye gaze. Both real partners and pictures were utilized to emphasize that information may be gathered without verbal interaction, gestures, or proximity. Keep in mind that the ability to "read" non-verbal social information is the foundation on which Theory of Mind (ToM) is developed.

You can foster continued development of this skill at home with the following activities:

- Organize a "treasure hunt" by hiding a favorite item somewhere in the room. Instruct the child to use your eyes as clues and ask, "Where are my eyes telling you to look?" Recognizing that another person has perceptual contact with an object will help to answer the child's targeted social questions. Try not to speak once the activity has begun. If necessary, make your eye gaze exaggerated and easier to follow for the first few turns. Alternate roles and let your child's eyes guide you to the hidden treasure.

- Use story books and magazines to draw your child's attention to drawings and photographs. Ask your child to read the character's facial expressions and body language to guess what they want, what they are thinking, or how they feel. Pay careful attention to both person clues and clues within the setting (where are they, what is going on around them). Ask your child, "How do you know?" to encourage him or her to point out the clues that led to the answers.

IMITATION: THE HEART OF SOCIAL DEVELOPMENT

Studies indicate that children who have social-communication conditions exhibit impairment in the spontaneous use of imitation for social gain. Early in development, children imitate a variety of models including actual people, characters as described in stories, and fictional characters who are portrayed in movies and television shows. By 18 months, delayed imitation emerges in the child's play as she incorporates actions that she has previously observed. After 24 months, the child will combine various delayed actions to create play themes from earlier, observed actions such as pretending to prepare a meal for the family or putting the doll in timeout. The ability for the child to represent meaningful experiences at a later time influences her understanding of causal relationships, ignites problem-solving abilities, and expands her knowledge of the social world. The imitation of models can also have a profound effect on the child's developing attitudes, beliefs, and emotional disposition.

Imitation plays a crucial role in the connection of cognition, behavior, and environment as a triadic process that mediates learning throughout development. Delays in the social form of imitation may pose a significant disruption in the development of maturing peer relationships through childhood and into adolescence.

Today's activities have focused on imitation for the purpose of social learning. Social imitation teaches the child to take a spontaneous role of leader and follower, eventually integrating both in a flexible, reciprocal system of responsiveness to a partner. You can strengthen your child's social imitation skills with the following activities at home:

- Play a game of "Mime." You will make the motions that your child will follow. Liken your child's role as a "mirror" and she or he should do exactly what they see you do. These types of unpredictable interactions increase the child's attention to non-verbal behaviors and will lead to improved generalization of social-imitation skills.

- Stand or sit next to your child while facing a mirror. Take turns making various facial expressions, some silly, some showing emotions. This will help children whose facial expressions do not consistently match their feelings or a given situation. If necessary, point out the action of specific body parts in concrete terms (i.e. "I am sad. My eyebrows are going up and my mouth is curving down").

LEAVING EGOCENTRISM

Preschool-aged children often assume that everyone else thinks as they do, has the same feelings as they do, and want the same things as they do. This reflects the child's inability to shift his mental perspective to differentiate his view from another. His thoughts and communications are typically about himself. However, soon after preschool, the child will develop the cognitive resources to make judgments about differing points of view.

Children who exhibit delays in social cognition commonly demonstrate a weakness in the ability to consider that other people's thoughts, beliefs, desires, and knowledge may differ from their own. This inability to appreciate the many different viewpoints of others has been long referred to as "egocentrism." Researchers suggest that this naïve egocentrism may follow some individuals well into adulthood and across their lifespan. This is most noticeable when the child has difficulty seeing the "big picture" in daily life and social situations.

The activities in this lesson have exposed your child to the various points of view that other people may have in relation to one subject. In addition, it has encouraged your child to consider other people's desires, thoughts, and opinions to compare and contrast them to his own. You can further enhance these skills at home with the following activities:

- Have a mealtime discussion about likes and dislikes. Choose a topic, such as "Favorite foods" and have each member of the family name a favorite food and then ask the others if they like or dislike it.

- Create a "Family favorites" booklet. Have your child dedicate one page to each person in the family and highlight favorite people, places, foods, games, movies, etc. Use drawings, photos, or magazine pictures to create the collages. Your child's ability to accurately differentiate the interests of others from his own is a good indication that perspective-taking skills are emerging.

MAKING PREDICTIONS

The ability to infer has been identified as a predictor of language and reading comprehension. Inference is a skill that allows the child to make reasonable predictions or conclusions that are based on what the child sees (in pictures), knows (from past experiences), and thinks (making connections). Children use inference to make sense of their social world and the literary world. Inference skills play an important role in the development of reading comprehension. The deficit in ToM is evident in two primary areas of development: social language development and reading comprehension. Within both contexts, it is not uncommon for children to understand and answer questions about specific details without understanding the big picture of a story or social scenario. Inference for the purpose of both social and text connections is made possible when the child is motivated by curiosity and question asking. Relatively any question that is not literal will lead us to making an inference. When a child engages in a process of thought to derive a plausible guess, she is able to answer the question, "How do you know?"

The activities in today's session provided a fun, interactive way to teach participants to search for important clues, use past experiences, and consider known information to make good, supported guesses. You can extend these lessons at home with the following activity:

- Read a story without words and have your child look for clues in the pictures to first make inferences about what the characters might be saying or thinking to create imaginary text and second to make predictions about what will happen on the next page. Have your child dictate the text while you write the words. This activity is an amazing opportunity for you to gain an awareness of your child's ability to really think.

If you go to the library to check out books, make a prediction about the behavior of people in the library. Ask, "How do you know?" to encourage your child to express her thought process.

Here are some great choices for teaching these concepts:

The Umbrella by Jan Brett

Good Dog, Carl by Alexandra Day

A Ball for Daisy by Chris Raschka

I Want My Hat Back by Jon Klassen

Mr. Men series by Roger Hargreaves

Chalk by Bill Thomson

Where is the Cake by T.T. Khing

The Red Book by Barbara Lehman

The Secret Box by Barbara Lehman

Little Miss series by Roger Hargreaves

THE IMPORTANCE OF PRETENSE

The importance of pretend play in early childhood development has been well documented and marked by well-known theorists of child development including Piaget, Bandura, and Vygotsky. Pretend play emerges from the child's evolving imitation skills and develops into themes and cooperative role play interactions. The absence of pretense may serve as a predictor of later challenges in perspective taking and ToM development. Role play, in particular, allows the child to imagine himself in a specific situation and act "as if" he were someone else. For example, if the child was to pretend to play "schools," he would need to think about how the teacher would act, sound, and interact with the imaginary students.

Professionals frequently call attention to the weakness of abstract thought processes across the spectrum. Imagination and creative thought are managed in the same part of the brain as abstract thinking. Imagining requires thinking that is counterfactual, or rather a substitution for what is real. This ability to employ the abstract in pretend play is a key element of social development. Watch children engage in pretend play and you will witness anything but reality. From mud pies that taste delicious to a stick used as a magic wand, pretend play allows for the child's imagination to take flight. Although this may seem like simple child's play, theorists have credited the hierarchy of play skills as the foundation of socialization, cognition, and self-regulation.

Children who exhibit delays in social development may seem undermotivated to engage in pretend play alone or as a synchronic unit with another child. They may become overwhelmed when dramatic play becomes more complex and choose to isolate with a more concrete, structured form of play.

The activities in today's lesson highlighted the elements of spontaneity and flexibility as they are typically represented in natural pretend play. You can support continued development of pretend play skills at home with the following activities:

- Take turns with your child acting "as if" you were another family member or familiar person. Pay careful attention to mimic the unique characteristics of another person (voice, laugh, frequent sayings).

- Encourage your child to find a symbolic use for various objects around the house. For example, pretend that a stick is a baseball bat, a banana is a telephone, and a shoe is a skateboard.

ASKING QUESTIONS

The research of Robert and Lynn Koegel emphasizes the critical role of self-initiated queries in the development of language and social pragmatics. They identified self-initiations as one of the primary target skills in their Pivotal Response Treatment approach. Question-asking behavior is commonly lacking when children exhibit delays in social development and yet, it is essential to the success of a social conversation. Clinical observation indicates that these children may be limited in their ability to engage in a reciprocal conversation.

Early in child development, question-asking behavior serves multiple purposes. Questions lead to learning, enhance expressive language, and satisfy the child's inner curiosities about the world. Answers to questions are stored in the child's memory and help to build those schemas (frameworks of information) that are necessary to help the child to organize and perceive new information.

Today's activities introduced flexible thinking in question asking. Your child engaged in various initiations while considering many possible questions related to a given topic or situation. You can foster continued development and variety in your child's self-initiations at home with the following activity:

- Choose several topics for mealtime "talk and share." Once a topic is identified, have each person keep the question-asking in play by asking questions related to the topic until the topic is exhausted. Your family members serve as excellent models of question-asking options, which enhances your child's repertoire of appropriate topic-related questions.

  Example: Topic = Movies

  ○ "Did you see…?"

  ○ "I really liked that movie. Did you?"

  ○ "Do we have that movie here at the house?"

  ○ "Did you see part one and two?"

  ○ "What was your favorite part of the movie?"

  ○ "Have you seen any other good movies lately?"

TWO-SIDED CONVERSATIONS

Once a child receives a response to a social question, she is likely to be encouraged to ask another question, add a comment, or share an emotion with her partner(s). This reciprocal exchange of verbal and non-verbal information constitutes a conversation. Clinical observations suggest that children who have delays in social-communication skills exhibit impairments in the behavior required to engage in successful conversations and may prefer one-sided talk. Studies have indicated that appropriate training can lead to the acquisition of conversational skills such as turn taking, enhanced understanding of mental states, novel response substitution, and non-verbal intentions. As children age, conversations become more important and complex, requiring the ability to shift attention and topics in a flexible manner.

Today's activities were chosen to teach your child to think flexibly when engaging in conversations by considering many possible questions, responses, and shifts related to a given topic. Last week's home activities provided an excellent introduction to conversational skills. You can extend skill development at home by adding these activities:

- Employ the use of a sibling or other peer partner to practice last week's question-asking game. To simulate the flow of a conversation, use a beach ball to roll back and forth between communicating partners. Have your child choose a topic for conversation and write it on the ball with a dry erase marker. Remind your child to "Check in" with the person talking (the ball will provide an additional visual aide). Take turns choosing a topic for variety.

- Use the term "Check in" to have your child respond immediately to a social partner with improved eyes and posture. We have been working on this in our sessions.

POINT OF VIEW AND PERSPECTIVE TAKING

During early development, a child is experiencing an enormous growth in his social awareness. By age four, the child is beginning to gain an understanding of his own feelings, ways to express emotions, ways to respond to emotions, and causes of his own feelings and the feelings of others. Social perception involves the integration of various skills:

- sustained attention

- behavioral regulation

- consideration of self/other thoughts

- shifting.

For the purpose of laying a basic foundation of perspective taking, two forms of this skill were highlighted in today's lesson. Visual perspective taking occurs when the child recognizes that another person has a different line of sight of an object. This perceptual level thinking refers to what the child can "see" versus what the other person can "see" from different points of view (sight). Social perspective taking occurs when the child recognizes that his own mental states differ from another person's. This conceptual level thinking refers to what the child "thinks, knows, believes" versus what another person "thinks, knows, believes" about the same thing.

You can enhance perspective-taking skills at home with the following activities:

- Play a hide and seek game that will test your child's understanding of false beliefs. Have your child show another person where an object is hidden. Ask that person to leave the room and have your child hide the object in a different location. Before the person returns, ask your child, "Where do you think she or he will look for the (object)?" Help your child to develop the awareness that his or her knowledge differs from the other person's. Probe questions might include:

  - "Does…know that you moved the object?"

  - "Did…see you move the object?"

  - "Does…know what you know?"

- Make opportunities available for your child to sit facing you while holding a book, deck of cards, or photos. Ask him or her to show it to you and see if your child turns the item in such a way that you can see what she or he was seeing. Your child's consistent ability to do this indicates that they are considering your point of view.

COOPERATIVE PLAY

Cooperative play is an essential stage of child development wherein important life skills are learned. When children are playing together, they are working, planning, sharing, taking on roles, engaging creativity, problem-solving, and developing relationships. Cooperative play enhances language development and teaches children about cultural society. Together, children ignite big-picture thinking.

Children who present with social and communication delays may have difficulty understanding how to coordinate their play with others. If they are unable to sustain attention to dynamic and flexible play interactions, they may choose to play alone. Cooperative play typically involves shifting, unpredictability, and abstract or imaginary themes.

In today's activities, your child learned about "We Play." This is a concrete term that is given to cooperative play to help your child to discriminate between isolated and joint or interactive play. You can review these terms at home and encourage your child to set goals to increase his "We Play" time with siblings or peers.

Me Play	We Play
Child is playing alone.	Children are playing together.
Child is not sharing toys.	Children are sharing the toys.
Child is not "checked in."	Child is looking at others.
Child is turned away.	Child is helping another child.
Child does not notice how the others feel.	Children are laughing together.

Video self-assessment is a powerful method to allow the child to observe and critique his own behavior. Children who have social challenges do not likely have many opportunities to actually observe themselves as they interact with others. Take a video of your child at play and review it at a later time. Pause the video frequently and ask your child if he is engaging in "Me Play" or "We Play." Your child will likely be more aware of his play behavior and alter it when he knows that it is being recorded.

GENERALIZATION

The skills that have been rehearsed during this program present a good foundation for increasing social cognition, self-awareness, and ultimately…Theory of Mind (ToM). However, maintenance and continued review of this program's language, activities, and concepts will be critical in ensuring your child's continued social success.

A list of recommended reading has been provided to help you to access resources that will enhance your child's continued development of ToM and address later stages in social development.

Your child's Self-Assessment Worksheet from today's session is also attached. Please review it with your child to identify areas of strength and weakness in our Me Play vs. We Play video assessment. You are encouraged to continue with video self-assessments as a beneficial method to teach your child to recognize and correct her own social behavior.

In addition, a pre-post test form has been provided to show you the specific skills that your child has mastered an understanding of and areas that may benefit from additional guidance.

Final Summary:

APPENDIX C

PARENT SOCIAL QUESTIONNAIRE

PARENT SOCIAL QUESTIONNAIRE

Child's Full Name:_____

DOB: _____   Age: _____

Parent(s) Name: _____

Address: _____   Zip: _____

Home Phone: _____ Work: _____ Cell: _____

Email: _____   Emergency Contact: _____

Siblings?:   ___yes ____ no   Ages?: _____

School: _____   Grade: _____

Has your child received any diagnosis (Please specify): _____

Please list any medications and the dosage that your child is taking:_____

_____

Does your child have any allergies? Please list:_____

_____

_____

What are your primary concerns regarding your child's social skills?: _____

_____

_____

What are your goals for your child?:_____

_____

_____

Reason for referral

Please tick the primary reason(s) for seeking social skills treatment (check all that apply):

☐ Difficulty making or maintaining friendships

☐ Difficulty reading non-verbal cues in others

☐ Difficulty managing frustration or stress

☐ Difficulty communicating with peers

☐ Difficulty joining in appropriate play with a peer or group of peers

Please tick any of the following that are a challenge for your child:

- ☐ Recognizing and responding to partner's feelings
- ☐ Cooperative play and collaborating with peers
- ☐ Initiating a social activity or conversation with a partner(s)
- ☐ Engaging in conversational turn taking
- ☐ Sustaining and shifting eye contact/body posture across speaking partners in a group
- ☐ Topic selection and maintenance (know how to stay on topic or switch topic in response to partner's interests during conversations)
- ☐ Recalling the sequence and highlights of social activities after a lapse of time
- ☐ Self-regulating to give appropriate attention and use self control in social situations
- ☐ Asking questions to gain information about a social partner's interests
- ☐ Exhibiting an understanding and compliance during games with social rules
- ☐ Assisting others when upset, hurt, or confused
- ☐ Recognizing and interpreting a partner's body language when bored, annoyed, or angry
- ☐ Coping with frustration
- ☐ Listening and sharing ideas, opinions, and comments with others
- ☐ Speaking with appropriate voice volume, speed, control
- ☐ Recognizing and demonstrating appropriate physical space and boundaries with partners
- ☐ Fleeting attention span (easily distracted or impulsive)
- ☐ Willingness to try new things (flexible thinking)
- ☐ Transitioning from one activity to another (leaving a preferred activity)
- ☐ Making or keeping friends at school
- ☐ Making or keeping friends in the community or neighborhood
- ☐ Interest in extracurricular activities
- ☐ Organizing language to "make good sense"
- ☐ Limited or extreme topics of interest

Recreational interests

What sports activities does your child enjoy?:_____

_____

How often does she or he do these activities?: _____

_____

_____

What hobbies does your child have?: _____

_____

_____

What are your child's special interests?: _____

_____

_____

Please list any areas of concern that have not been identified:_____

_____

_____

Thank you!

APPENDIX D

VIDEO CONSENT FORM

VIDEO CONSENT FORM

Child's name:_____

Video modeling is an integral component of this skill training program. It is used for the comparison of pre-post treatment outcomes and for self-monitoring by participants.

By signing this form I give permission to _____
and any of its participating clinicians to videotape sessions for the following purpose(s):

- For review by the clinicians for the purpose of participant self-monitoring, tracking progress, and group feedback.

- For educational purposes to teach theory and techniques of intervention to professionals in health-related fields (i.e. mental health, pediatrics, education, occupational therapy, physical therapy, speech and language therapy).

I understand I may withdraw my permission at any time.

Parent/Guardian name (please print): _____

Parent/Guardian signature: _____

Date: _____

APPENDIX E

SKILL ASSESSMENT SCALE

SKILL ASSESSMENT SCALE

Target skill	Pre	Post	Comments
Respond to gesture			
Eye gaze detection and following			
Imitation			
Point of view			
Joint attention (triadic social interaction)			
Symbolic play			
Pretend role play			
Contents false belief test			
Self-initiations			

Responses to these target skills were not prompted in any way. The instructor has recorded a + if the child independently demonstrated the skill and a – if the child responded incorrectly or did not respond at all.

APPENDIX F

TARGET SKILL PARADIGM

TARGET SKILL PARADIGM

Target skill	Example
Respond to a gesture	The partner will attempt to gain the child's attention by calling his or her name and extending a point in the direction of the item of interest.
Eye gaze detection and following	The partner indicates the location of a hidden object through eye gaze.
Imitation	The partner asks the child to "Copy me" while modeling various facial expressions (happy, sad, angry, surprised feelings) and demonstrating movements (reaching, tapping, clapping, peek-a-boo). The child is scored on his or her ability to imitate all actions.
Point of view	The child is asked to identify a favorite food, toy, or television show. The partner will ask the child, "What do you think is my favorite...?" for each category. The child is scored on his or her ability to recognize that he or she cannot assume the answer.
Joint attention (triadic social interaction)	Partner demonstrates the "element of surprise" (i.e. blow a balloon and let it go, jack-in-the-box toy, knock over a tower of blocks). The child is scored on triadic interaction (looking at the object, partner, and back to the object).
Symbolic play	The child is shown several objects and asked, "What could this be?" Examples: banana = phone, pencil = fork, plate = hat, tube = telescope. The child is scored on his or her ability to pretend to use the objects to symbolize something else.
Pretend role play	The child is asked to pretend to act like a monkey, adult, child in a candy store, and person on a rollercoaster for the first time. The child is scored on his or her ability to exhibit actions or mannersims that are characteristic of the identified role.
Contents false belief test	The child sees a crayon box with a button inside. She or he is asked, "Here is a crayon box, what do you think is inside?" She or he is shown the button. She or he is shown a toy figure named Tom. Tom has never seen inside the box. The child is asked, "What does Tom think is inside the box?"
Self-initiations	The partner will ask various questions of the child and initiate a conversation about a topic of interest to the child. The child will be scored on his or her ability to initiate social questions of the partner or peer for the purpose of gaining information about the partner's interests, roles, purpose, family, experiences, etc.

Responses to these target skills should not be prompted in any way. The instructor will record a + if the child independently demonstrated the skill and a – if she or he responded incorrectly or did not respond at all.

APPENDIX G

WHAT MAKES ME FEEL

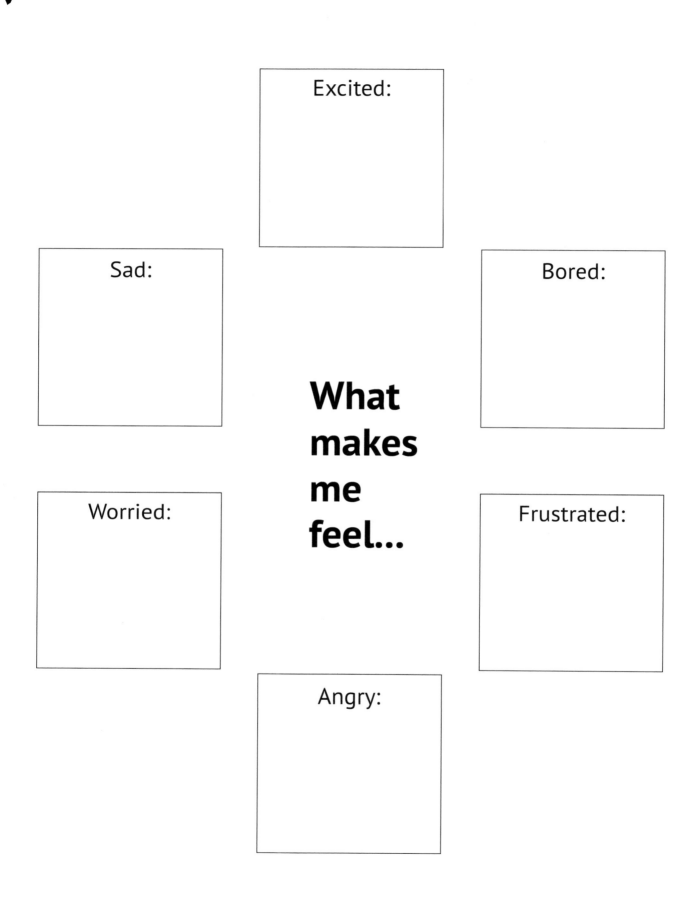

Excited:

Sad:

Bored:

Worried:

What makes me feel...

Frustrated:

Angry:

ALIKE AND DIFFERENT COMPARISON SHEET

ALIKE AND DIFFERENT COMPARISON SHEET

	Me	(A person in my family)	My instructor
Favorite movies			
Favorite foods			
Favorite people			
Favorite places			

APPENDIX I

VENN DIAGRAM WORKSHEET

VENN DIAGRAM WORKSHEET

Topic: _____

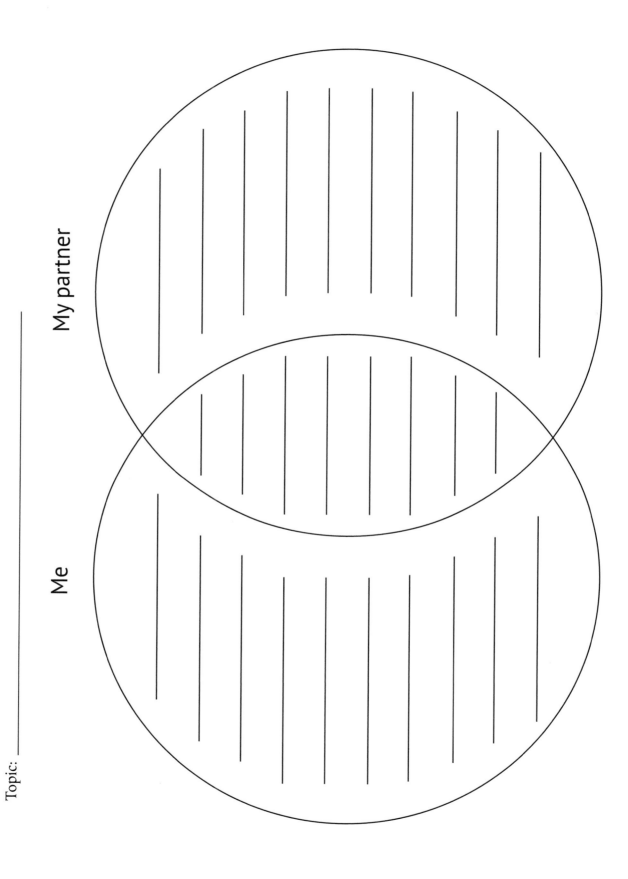

My partner

Me

APPENDIX J

QUESTIONS PROMPT SHEET

QUESTIONS PROMPT SHEET

What?   Do you...?

Who?   Where?

Is...?   Can you...?

Are you...?   Why?

APPENDIX K

QUESTION WEB WORKSHEET

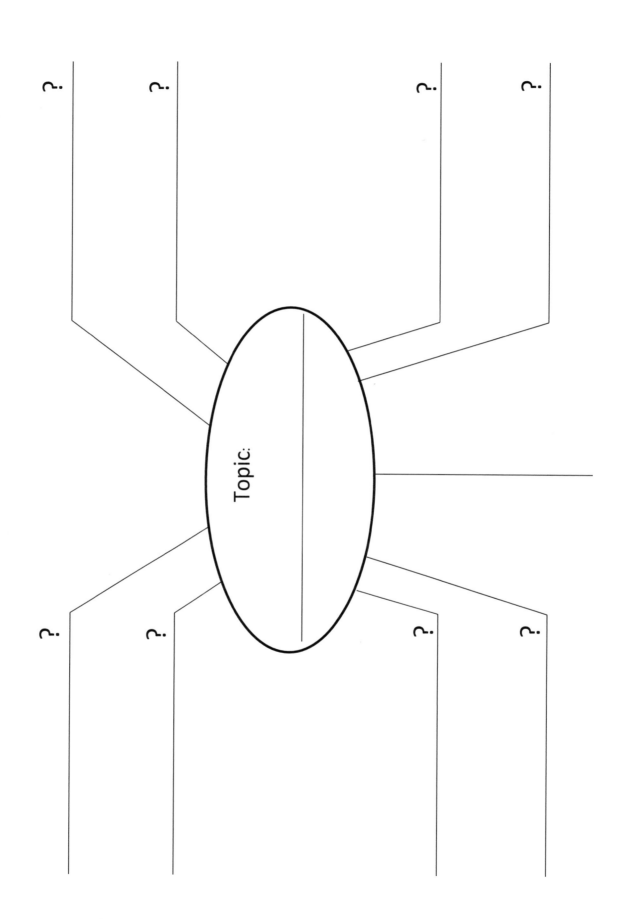

QUESTION WEB WORKSHEET

Topic:

?. ?. ?. ?.

?. ?. ?. ?.

APPENDIX L

CHATTER LADDER WORKSHEET

CHATTER LADDER WORKSHEET

Topic:

APPENDIX M

SELF-ASSESSMENT WORKSHEET

SELF-ASSESSMENT WORKSHEET

How did I do?

Mark a + if the video shows that I am doing the skill.

Mark a − if the video shows that I am not doing the skill.

Checked in with my eyes	
Checked in with my body	
I am doing "We" Play	

RECOMMENDED READING

THEORY OF MIND

Baron-Cohen, Simon (1995) *MindBlindness: An Essay on Autism and Theory of Mind.* Cambridge, MA: MIT Press.

Doherty, Martin J. (2009) *Theory of Mind: How Children Understand Thoughts and Feelings.* New York, NY: Psychology Press.

Garcia-Winner, Michelle and Madrigal, Stephanie (2008) *SuperFlex…A Super Hero Social Thinking Curriculum.* San Jose, CA: Think Social Publishing.

Garcia-Winner, Michelle (2006) *Think Social! A Social Thinking Curriculum for School-Aged Students for Teaching Social Thinking and Related Skills to Students with High Functioning Autism PDD-NOS, Asperger's Syndrome, Non-verbal Learning Disorder, and ADHD.* San Jose, CA: Think Social Publishing.

Howlin, Patricia, Baron-Cohen, Simon, and Hadwin, Julie A. (1999) *Teaching Children with Autism to Mind Read: A Practical Guide for Teachers and Parents.* Chichester, John Wiley & Sons.

SELF-REGULATION

Dunn-Buron, Kari (2012) *The Incredible Five Point Scale.* Lenexa, KS: AAPC Publishing.

Sautter, Elizabeth and Wilson, Kristen (2011) *Whole Body Listening Larry at Home.* San Jose, CA: Think Social Publishing.

Sautter, Elizabeth and Wilson, Kristen (2011) *Whole Body Listening Larry at School.* San Jose, CA: Think Social Publishing.

Shellenberger, Sherry and Williams, Mary Sue (1996) *How Does Your Engine Run? The Alert Program for Self Regulation.* Alburquerque, NM: Therapy Works Inc.

Shellenberger, Sherry and Williams, Mary Sue (2001) *Take Five! Staying Alert at Home and School.* Alburquerque, NM: Therapy Works Inc.

PEER SENSITIVITY TRAINING

Kraus, Jeanne (2004) *Cory Stories: A Kid's Book about Living with ADHD.* Washington DC: Magination Press.

Ordetx, Michael (2011) *Understanding Autism: A Sensitivity Training Guide for Kids Like Me.* Sarasota, FL: The Peppertree Press.

Welton, Jude (2003) *Can I tell you about Asperger's Syndrome?* London: Jessica Kingsley Publishers.

REFERENCES

Antonietti, A., Liverta-Sempio, O., and Machetti, A. (2006) *Theory of Mind and Language in Developmental Contexts*. New York, NY: Springer.

Astington, J.W., and Jenkins, J.M. (1999) "A longitudinal study of the relationship between language and theory of mind development." *Developmental Psychology 35*, 1311–1320.

Bandura, A. (1971) *Social Learning Theory*. New York, NY: General Learning Press.

Bandura, A. (1989) "Social Cognitive Theory." In R. Vasta (ed.) *Annals of Child Development. Vol. 6. Six Theories of Child Development*. Greenwich, CT: JAI Press.

Baron-Cohen, S. (2001) *Mindblindness: An Essay on Autism and Theory of Mind*. Cambridge, MA: MIT Press.

Baron-Cohen, S., Leslie, A., and Frith, U. (1986) "Mechanical, behavioral and intentional understanding of picture stories in autistic children." *British Journal of Developmental Psychology 4,* 113–125.

Bergen, D., and Mauer, D. (2000) "Symbolic Play, Phonological Awareness, and Literacy Skills at Three Age Levels." In K.A. Roskos and J.F. Christie (eds) *Play and Literacy in Early Childhood: Research from Multiple Perspectives*. New York, NY: Erlbaum.

Carr, E., Dewitz, P., and Patberg, J. (1989) "Using cloze for inference training with expository text." *The Reading Teacher 42*, 6, 380–385.

Charlop-Christy, M.H., and Daneshvar, S. (2003) "Using video modeling to teach perspective taking to children with autism." *Journal of Positive Behavior Interventions 5*, 12–21.

Charlop, M.H., and Milstein, J.P. (1989) "Teaching autistic children conversational speech using video modeling." *Journal of Applied Behavior Analysis 22*, 275–285.

Charlop, M.H., Dennis, B., Carpenter, M.H., and Greenberg, A.L. (2010) "Teaching socially expressive behaviors to children with autism through video modeling." *Education and Treatment of Children 33*, 3, 371–393.

Charman, T., Baron-Cohen, S., Swettenham, J., Baird, G., Cox, A., and Drew, A. (2000) "Testing joint attention, imitation, and play as infancy precursors to language and theory of mind." *Cognitive Development 15*, 481–498.

Eckerman, C.O., and Stein, M.R. (1990) "How imitation begets imitation and toddlers' generation of games." *Developmental Psychology 26,* 3, 370–378.

Epley, N., Morewedge, C.K., and Keysar, B. (2004) "Perspective taking in children and adults: Equivalent egocentrism but differential correction." *Journal of Experimental Social Psychology 40*, 760–768.

Frith, U. (2012) "Why we need cognitive explanations of autism, 38 Bartlett Lecture 2010." *Quarterly Journal of Experimental Psychology 65*, 11, 2073–2092.

Frith, U., and Frith, C. (2001) "The biological basis of social interaction." *Current Directions in Psychological Science 10*, 151–155.

Frith, U., and Frith, C. (2003) "Development and neurophysiology of Mentalizing." *Philosophical transactions of the Royal Society of London, Series B, Biological Sciences*. March 29; 358, 459–73.

Frith, U., and de Vignemont, F. (2005) "Egocentrism, allocentrism, and asperger syndrome." *Consciousness and Cognition 14*, 719–738.

Gately, S.E. (2008) "Facilitating reading comprehension for students on the autism spectrum." *Teaching Exceptional Children 40*, 3, 40–45.

Goldman, A.I. (2006) *Simulating Minds: The Philosophy, Psychology, and Neuroscience of Mindreading*. New York, NY: Oxford University Press.

Gopnik, A., and Astington, J.W. (1988) "Children's understanding of representational change and its relation to the understanding of false-belief and the appearance reality distinction." *Child Development 59*, 26–37.

Gopnik, A., and Meltzoff, A.N. (1994) "Minds, Bodies, and Persons: Young Children's Understanding of the Self and Others as Reflected in Imitation and Theory of Mind Research." In M.L. Boccia (ed.) *Self-Awareness in Animals and Humans: Developmental Perspectives.* New York, NY: Cambridge University Press.

Gray, C. (1994) *Comic Strip Conversations: Illustrating Interactions that Teach Conversation Skills to Children with Autism.* Texas: Future Horizons Ltd.

Grice, S., Halit, H., Farroni, T., Baron-Cohen, S., Bolton, P., and Johnson, M.H. (2005) "Neural correlates of eye gaze detection in young children with autism." *Cortex 41*, 342–353.

Harris, P.L., and Jalloul, M. (2012) "Running on empty? Observing causal relationships of play and development." *American Journal of Play 6*, 1.

Iacoboni, M.,Woods, R.P., Brass, M., Bekkering, H., Mazziotta, J.C., and Rizzolatti, G. (1999) "Cortical mechanisms of human imitation." *Science 286*, 2526–2528.

Iland, E. (2011) *Drawing a Blank: Improving Comprehension for Readers on the Autism Spectrum.* Kansas, KS: AAPC Publishing.

Ingersoll, B. (2008) "The social role of imitation in autism." *Infants and Young Children 21*, 2, 107–119.

Jahromi, L.B., Bryce, C., and Swanson, J. (2013) "The importance of self-regulation for the school and peer engagement of children with high-functioning autism." *Research in Autism Spectrum Disorders 7*, 235–246.

Kanter, C. (2006) "Children's imaginary play: A descriptive psychology approach. Advances in Descriptive Psychology." *Advances in Descriptive Psychology 9*, 257–286.

Kim, J.A., Szatmari, P., Bryson, S.E., Streiner, D.L., and Wilson, F.J. (2000) "The prevalence of anxiety and mood problems among children with autism and asperger's syndrome." *Autism 4*, 2, 117–132.

Koegel, L.K., Carter, C.M., and Koegel, R.L. (2003) "Teaching children with autism self initiations as a pivotal response." *Topics in Language Disorders 23*, 2, 134–145.

Langdell, T. (1978) "Recognition of faces: An approach to the study of autism." *Journal of Child Psychology and Psychiatry 19*, 255–268.

Leekam, S., Baron-Cohen, S., Perrett, D., Milders, M., and Brown, S. (1997) "Eye-direction detection: A dissociation between geometric and joint attention skills in autism." *British Journal of Developmental Psychology 15*, 77–95.

Leekam, S.R., Hunnisett, E., and Moore, C. (1998) "Targets and cues: Gaze-following in children with autism." *Journal of Child Psychology and Psychiatry 39*. 951–962.

Leslie, A. (1987) "Pretence and representation: The origins of 'theory of mind'." *Psychological Review 94*, 412–426.

Leslie, A., and Frith, U. (1988) "Autistic children's understanding of seeing, knowing, and believing." *British Journal of Developmental Psychology 6*, 315–324.

Lewis, C., and Mitchell, P. (2014) *Children's Early Understanding of Mind.* Hove, UK: Psychology Press.

Lombardo, M.V., Chakrabarti, B., Bullmore, E.T., Sadek, S.A., *et al.* (2010) "Atypical neural self-representation in autism." *Brain 133*, 2, 611–624.

Lord, C. (1995) "Follow-up of two-year-olds referred for possible autism." *Journal of Child Psychology and Psychiatry 36*, 8, 1365–1382.

Loveland, K. (2005) "Social-emotional Impairment and Self-Regulation in Autism Spectrum Disorders." In J. Nadel and D. Muir (eds) *Typical and Impaired Emotional Development.* Oxford: Oxford University Press.

Marsh, L.E., and Hamilton, C. (2011) "Dissociation of mirroring and mentalising systems in autism." *Neuroimage 56*, 1511–1519.

Meltzoff, A.N., and Brooks, R. (2007) "Eyes Wide Shut: The Importance of Eyes in Infant Gaze Following and Understanding Other Minds." In R. Flom, K. Lee and D. Muir (eds) *Gaze Following: Its Development and Significance.* Mahwah, NJ: Erlbaum.

Mundy, P., and Newell, L. (2007) "Attention, joint attention, and social cognition." *Current Directions in Psychological Science, 16*, 5, 269–274.

Neilsen, M., and Dissanayake, C. (2004) "Pretend play, mirror self recognition, and imitation: A longitudinal investigation through the second year." *Infant Behavior and Development 27*, 342–365.

Ossorio, P.G. (2006) *The Behavior of Persons.* Ann Arbor, MI: Descriptive Psychology Press.

Osterling, J., and Dawson, G. (1994) "Early recognition of children with autism: A study of first birthday home videotapes." *Journal of Autism and Developmental Disorders 24*, 247–257.

Perner, J., Leeham, S.R., and Wimmer, H. (1987) "Three year olds difficulty with false belief: The case for a conceptual deficit." *British Journal of Developmental Psychology 39*, 437–471.

Piaget, J. (1962) *Play, Dreams, and Imitation in Childhood*. New York, NY: Norton.

Premack, D., and Woodruff, G. (1978) "Does the chimpanzee have a theory of mind?" *Behavior and Brain Sciences 1,* 4, 515–526.

Press, C., Richardson, D., and Bird, G. (2010) "Intact imitation of emotional facial actions in autism spectrum conditions." *Neuropsychologia 48*, 3291–3297.

Ramachandran, V.S., and Oberman, L.M. (2006) "Broken mirrors: A theory of autism." *Scientific American 17*, 20–29.

Randi, J., Newman, T., and Brigovenko, E. (2010) "Teaching children with autism to read for meaning: Challenges and possibilities." *Journal of Autism and Developmental Disorders 40*, 7, 890–902.

Repacholi, B., and Gopnik, A. (1997) "Early reasoning about desires: Evidence from 14–18 month olds." *Developmental Psychology 33*, 1, 12–21.

Rogers, S.J., Hepburn, S.L., Stackhouse, T., and Wehner, E. (2003) "Imitation performance in toddlers with autism and those with other developmental disorders." *Journal of Child Psychology and Psychiatry 44*, 5, 763–781.

Smith-Myles, B., Trautman, M.L., and Schelvan, R.L. (2004) *The Hidden Curriculum*. Shawnee Mission, KS: Autism Asperger Publishing.

Stone, W.L., and Yoder, P.J. (2001) "Predicting spoken language level in children with autism spectrum disorders." *Autism 5*, 341–361.

Striano, T., and Rochat, P. (2000) "Emergence of selective social referencing in infancy." *Infancy 1, 2*, 253–264.

Vygotsky, L.S. (1967) "Play and its role in the mental development of the child." *Soviet Psychology 5*, 3, 6–18.

Warnekan, F., and Tomasello, M. (2006) "Altruistic help in human infants and young chimpanzees." *Science 3*, 11, 1301–1303.

Wellman, H. (1990) *The Child's Theory of Mind*. Cambridge, MA: MIT Press.

Wellman, H.M., Cross, D., and Watson, J. (2001) "Meta-analysis of theory of mind development: The truth about false belief." *Child Development 72*, 655–684.

Wellman, H. and Lui, D. (2004) "Scaling of theory of mind tasks," *Child Development 75 (2)*, 523–41.

Wetherby, A., and Prutting, C. (1984) "Profiles of communicative and cognitive-social abilities in autistic children." *Journal of Speech and Hearing Resources 27*, 3, 364–377.

White, A.H. (2004) Cognitive behavioural therapy in children with autistic spectrum disorder. http://ww.autismfor-us.org/INFO-OTHERS/Cognitive%20behavioural%20therapy%20in%20children%20with%20autistic%20spectrum%20disorder.pdf, accessed 08 August 2014.

Wimmer, H., and Perner, J. (1983) "Beliefs about beliefs: Representation and constraining function of wrong beliefs in young children's understanding of deception." *Cognition 13*, 103–128.

Wolfberg, P.J., Bottema-Beutel, K., and DeWitt, M. (2012) "Including children with autism in social and imaginary play with typical peers." *American Journal of Play 5*, 1, 55–80.

Wolfberg, P.J., and Schuler, A.L. (1993) "Integrated play groups: A model for promoting the social and cognitive dimensions of play in children with autism." *Journal of Autism and Developmental Disorders 23*, 467–489.

Wulff, S.B. (1985) "The symbolic and object play of children with autism: A review." *Journal of Autism and Developmental Disabilities 15*, 2, 139–148.

Yue Y., Yanjie S., and Chan, R. (2011) "The Relationship Between Visual Perspective Taking and Imitation Impairments in Children with Autism." In Dr. Mohammad-Reza Mohammadi (ed.) A Comprehensive Book on Autism Spectrum Disorders. Croatia, Intech.

   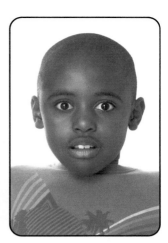

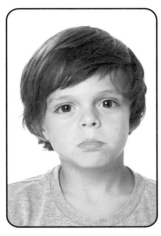   

 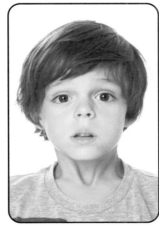

Angry   Angry   Angry   Angry

Angry   Angry   Bored   Bored

Bored   Bored   Bored   Bored

Confused   Confused   Confused   Confused

Confused	Confused	Excited	Excited
Excited	Excited	Excited	Excited
Frustrated	Frustrated	Frustrated	Frustrated
Frustrated	Frustrated	Sad	Sad

Sad

Sad

Sad

Sad

Worried

Worried

Worried

Worried

Worried

Worried

✓

| worried | worried | worried | worried |

| sad | sad | sad | sad |

| bored | bored | bored | bored |

| frustrated | frustrated | frustrated | frustrated |

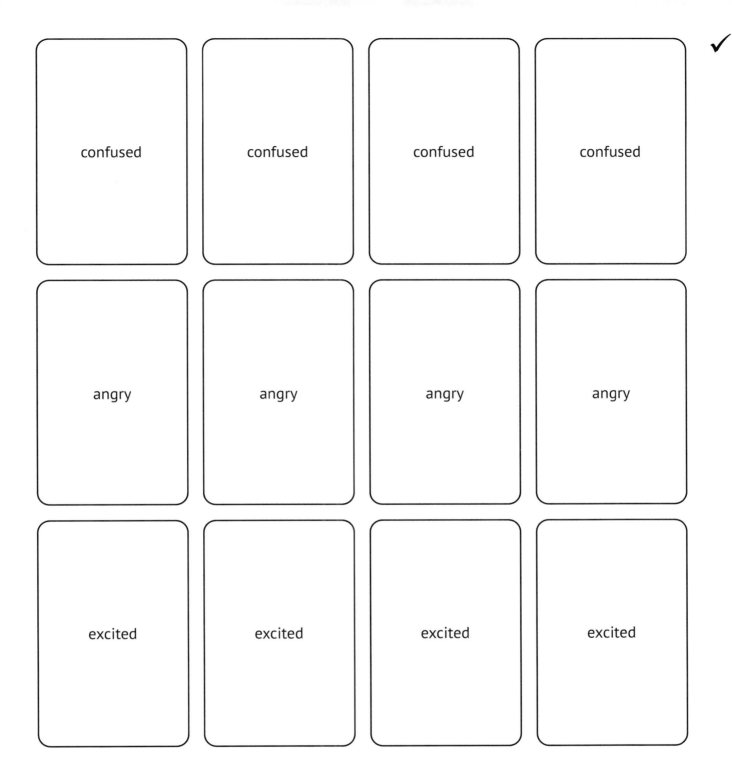

confused	confused	confused	confused
angry	angry	angry	angry
excited	excited	excited	excited

I am slimy to touch.

I slither on the ground.

I have a long, thin tongue.

I can be poisonous.

Who am I?

I move back and forth.

I have scales.

I live in the water.

I breathe through my gills.

Who am I?

I cannot walk.

I cannot use a fork or spoon.

I like to be held.

I cry to talk.

Who am I?

It is very quiet.

This is a big place.

There are thousands of words.

You can "check out" a good read.

Where am I?

I drive a truck.

I come to your house each day.

I leave something in your mailbox.

I take letters from your mailbox.

Who am I?

There are fruits and vegetables.

People come here each week.

You pay for what you take.

You put it all in a cart.

Where am I?

I have a tongue.

I have a lot of holes.

You tie laces over my tongue.

You stick your foot in me.

What am I?

I am slippery.

You rub me all over your body.

I stay in the bath or shower.

I make suds.

What am I?

I have soft fur.

I have a long tail.

I am afraid of cats.

I like to eat cheese.

Who am I?

I have a lot of seats in my back.

I am usually yellow.

My doors open and close.

I stop to let people on and off.

What am I?

You put me on the table.

You draw or write on me.

You can fold me.

You can turn me into an airplane.

What am I?

You can pop me open.

I come in many colors.

You hold me up high.

I keep you dry.

What am I?

Act "as if" you are a...
Teacher

Act "as if" you are a...
Baby

Act "as if" you are a...
Tree

Act "as if" you are a...
Fish just caught

Act "as if" you are a...
Grandparent

Act "as if" you are a...
Mouse hiding from a cat

Act "as if" you are a...
Librarian

Act "as if" you are...
Lost in the forest

As If Cards Set

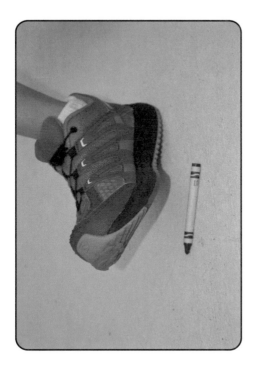